Audience of
ONE

Perfect Performance or Passionate Praise?

Jeremy and Connie Sinnott

Destiny Image® Publishers, Inc.
P.O. Box 310
Shippensburg, PA 17257-0310

"Speaking to the Purposes of God for This Generation
and for the Generations to Come"

ISBN 0-7684-2014-8

For Worldwide Distribution
Printed in the U.S.A.

This book and all other Destiny Image, Revival Press,
and Treasure House books are available
at Christian bookstores and distributors worldwide.

To place a book order, call toll free **1-800-722-6774**.
For more information on foreign distributors,
call **717-532-3040**.
Or reach us on the Internet: **http://www.destinyimage.com**

Dedication

This book is dedicated to our friends all over the globe who have joined us in seeking God's face and to our three sons, Shawn, Trevor, and Luke, who have persevered with us over the years and who minister alongside us.

Acknowledgments

There have been a number of people who have significantly impacted our lives and influenced our teaching. We thank God for these saints:

Jerry and Beryl Jeffs, spiritual parents who discipled us as young Christians and introduced us to the work of the Holy Spirit.

John and Carol Arnott, our friends and mentors who have implanted so much into our lives. They gave us grounding in understanding the Father heart of God, taking us with them in a fast learning curve, following the flow of the Holy Spirit.

John Wimber, through whose teaching in the Vineyard movement we have been made all the more aware of the magnitude of God's grace, mercy, and love.

John and Paula Sandford, who taught us the importance of being healed of the hurts of the past in order to receive the fullness of the Father's love.

Mark Virkler, who taught us how to discern God's voice more clearly and commune with Him more closely.

Endorsements

"*Audience of One* will help raise up worship leaders who will lead congregations into the throne room of God, where they will experience God's marvelous presence. This book will teach one how to 'flow' with the river of God in worship."

—Mark Virkler, Ph.D.
Author of *Communion With God*

"The voice of the Bridegroom calls us into a deeper, more intimate and passionate place of worship. This book will encourage you to open your heart that He might purify His Bride."

—Mike Bickle
Senior Pastor, Metro Christian Fellowship
Ministry Director, Friends of the Bridegroom

"Jeremy and Connie Sinnott have been my close friends and associates in ministry for over ten years.

They have been a crucial part of our Renewal team and are still my very favorite worship leaders. Their insights into the heart of becoming a worshiper of the living God are life-changing."

—John Arnott
Senior Pastor, Toronto Airport Christian Fellowship

"Jeremy and Connie Sinnott introduced me to the notion that we were created to worship, to tell God how much we love Him. In this book you'll find out that worship is one of the most important aspects of our lives from two people who personify the true and pure worshiper's heart not only in their music, but most of all in their lives."

—Dan Cutrona
President, Kle-Toi Records

Contents

Preface

In His mercy and grace, for the past few years our heavenly Father has been taking us on a journey in learning how to worship. We really want to know what it means to "worship in spirit and in truth" (Jn. 4:23).

When I (Jeremy)[1] was still a teenager, I met a group of evangelical Anglican young people who were on fire for Jesus and were absolutely free in their passion for Him. Through their example and care, and through His call, I gave my life to the Lord Jesus. My music focus radically changed from being a protest singer who was looking for a cause to being a lover of Jesus. Here was a much higher calling and a far greater reason for singing.

My wife, Connie, had grown up in the Church and had surrendered her life to Jesus as a child. Music and song had always been a normal way of life for her. One of the things I loved about her when we first met was that she was always humming a song—she still does. By the time we met, I had become a band member of that Anglican group (the Hakamu). Connie was drawn in by these youth who were excited about Jesus, and she joined the band as well.

The Lord has taken us from a place of using music to entertain and bless to using this medium to teach Christians how to worship. It didn't take us long to realize that we ourselves didn't really know how to worship. At first we thought that worship was just a matter of singing or leading songs, of practicing and organizing. Then the Langley worship team with Gary and Joy Best introduced us to the Vineyard model back in 1987, and we were changed forever. Intimate, passionate love songs captured our hearts. These were songs sung to the Lord, not just songs sung about Him.

God spoke to us in these songs, and He brought healing to our hearts and refreshment to our spirits. We were led into a new level of vulnerability. We began to listen to the leading of the Holy Spirit. "Performance" began to lift from our lives, and we began to become more like instruments prepared simply for His pleasure. We gave Him our agenda and earnestly looked for His. As we worshiped with increased passion, we found that His presence gently invaded.

In the outpouring of the Holy Spirit that began in January 1994 at the Toronto Airport Christian Fellowship, where I serve as worship leader, God began revealing His glory in our midst. We could hardly bear the sweetness of His love. How could we not worship with all that was within us? Having now tasted, our desire is that His Spirit will never lift. We can never go back to just singing songs, and we desire still greater intimacy and more of His presence.

As God's power and presence have been increasing worldwide, the intensity of His glory in worship has also been increasing. We realize that He is taking us somewhere. As He continues to call us deeper, we long for the glory that is yet to be revealed.

Whether you are a worship leader, a pastor, a worship team member, or a worshiper within a congregation, my wife and I have written this book with the hope that it will encourage you in your process of seeking God in deeper worship. My prayer is that in your worship experience you will begin to recognize yourself as part of the Body and Bride of Christ and that your songs will be sung for Him alone, your audience of One.

Foreword

Jeremy and Connie Sinnott have written a much needed book. Who among us has not grieved when worship leaders have "performed," leaving their congregations sidetracked? Or when worship leaders thought they had to intersperse their own thoughts and preachings until would-be worshipers felt like commuters standing on the dock watching the ferry pull away empty?! This book is a blessed antidote. Continually the Sinnotts urge us to involve everyone in worship; continually they stress that the entire congregation is the worship team.

The trite truism that "the messenger is the message" finds fresh life here. Paula and I have greatly enjoyed worshiping at Toronto Airport Christian Fellowship. We are so grateful that Jeremy practices what he has preached here. He listens afresh each moment to what the Holy Spirit wants in worship; he stays transparent so that people don't come away saying, "Oh, what a wonderful musician," but "Oh, what a wonderful Lord."

The down-to-earth, simple style of writing and the sweet graciousness of the Lord that radiates through the pages model what is taught: The text draws us into praying, worshiping, and experiencing Him firsthand. We suggest that you, the reader, not skim hurriedly, looking for gems, but slow down and feel the Holy Spirit in your own spirit, basking, heartfully praying through the prayers at the end of each chapter. Sense the heart of the Lord in the Sinnotts, and let that transparency carry you into private worship and then into the newness of love and exhilaration found in corporate worship. That's what it's all about, as God woos His people back to Himself from the hustle of today's hurry-hurry world.

Audience of One is aptly named. As Jeremy says so often and so well throughout, the only audience who matters in worship is our one true God and Father.

Today there is a glorious rediscovery of corporate worship. If it is not to miss the mark, however, the lessons of this book need to be heard, not only by every worship leader (this is a must-read, a prerequisite book for every "wannabe" worship leader), but also by all gatherings of Christians, until the quiet and gracious discipline that the Sinnotts espouse has become ingrained and easily operative wherever Christians enter His gates and trod His courts of worship.

We need to pray through the list of conditions that prevent intimacy (mentioned in the first chapter): fear, sin, discouragement, distractions, wrong theology, and hurts, especially in relation to our earthly fathers. How wonderful it would be if every worship leader were to learn and adhere to the respect of authority recommended in Chapter 4. What powerful intercession and spiritual warfare could result were all of us to come into the unity and humility of heart that Chapters 5 and 6 teach. And every gifted musician should pray the Abraham-Isaac prayer spoken of in Chapter 6, laying his gifts on the altar lest he serve and idolize the gift rather than the Lord.

We especially enjoyed how Jeremy testified so openly of how each new revelation and fresh outpouring from the Holy Spirit in the renewal broke open his denominationally conditioned mind and changed his heart and practices for the better.

Beyond learning our Lord's "new-old" way of worshiping, somehow we've all got to come into that security in God, into that trust and willingness to risk about which the Sinnotts testify throughout the book. We've got to stumble into—persevere—into the blind, childlike faith that alone will enable us to unfurl sails that won't rip and blow away in the new move of God that looms over the horizon. Ours has been a Gnostic faith: "Convince me intellectually and then I'll believe." The issue is not first theological or mental, but is the question, "Who's in control?"

Let readers see how often God sovereignly moved and continually upset Jeremy's practiced ways, plunging him again and again into the process of "crossed-out un-learning," as God yearned for a Jeremy who could let the Lord be the Lord. I guess because over the years I've learned to love Jeremy so much, my heart leaped up page after page to say, "Yes! He's learning it! He's dying. God is resurrecting His own." God is seeking a people who can let Him be God, who can let go of their controlling ways no matter what their place is in the Body. But I think Jeremy is right; it has to begin with those who lead in worship.

The final chapter, Chapter 8, speaks of "Worshipers in Process." Whatever we're called to do, whoever we are, that's who we are. Read the book, if you will, to become a better worship leader, but whatever office or non-office you hold, let it take you beyond into the beautiful process of daily dying to self (see Gal. 2:20; 5:24) and, coming up wet behind the ears, being ready to plunge in again. It happens first—and best—in worship.

John Sandford
The Elijah House
Post Falls, Idaho

A Festival of Joy

(Jeremy Sinnott)

We celebrate Your presence Lord.
We sing to You our song.
We celebrate with all our hearts,
The joy goes on and on.

We celebrate Your presence Lord,
Let fire fill this place.
We celebrate with lifted arms,
Come meet us face to face!

A festival of love,
A festival of joy,
A festival of peace,
Because of You!
[Repeat]

We lift Your name, Lord Jesus
In this place.
[Repeat 2x]

Forever more,
Forever more,
Forever more,
Forever more.

Introduction

As we come together to seek God's face, it is not our music that impresses Him. God looks into our hearts to find those who long to know Him. His desire is that we open ourselves up to Him so that He can pour in His healing love, reveal more of His presence, and empower our lives. In these days, when God has been pouring out His Spirit, He is taking the Church through a process. He is teaching us more about intercessory prayer, prophecy, the Father heart of God, healing of past hurts, repentance, holiness, and intimacy with Him. All these elements are issues of the heart. Since worship is also a matter of the heart, it has been deeply affected by all these things.

God has been taking us through different stages or seasons. He seems to be preparing us as we move closer to His end-time agenda. More than ever, God's people are learning the importance of hearing His voice for direction and the importance of cooperating with Him as He sets forth His strategies for these endtimes. Every Christian needs to step into his or her place, and as the pieces of the puzzle come together, His purposes will be revealed.

The Bride is being made ready for the coming of her Bridegroom. The end-time army is being equipped and prepared for service. The glory of the Lord has truly been rising upon us. What glorious days we live in! What a privilege is ours to witness the unfolding of God's plan. Our heavenly Father is pouring out His love and His wonderful Holy Spirit upon us. How can we not respond? It is our prayer that this book will be a tool that will help you to turn your face earnestly to seek His presence. May you be inspired to give your utmost in worship to your audience of One.

Jesus, I Long to Be Held

(Connie Sinnott)

Jesus, I long to be held in Your presence.
Jesus, I need You to draw me there;

To rest in Your embrace;
The touch of Your sweet caress,
Enfolded in tenderness,
In Your arms.

Oh how I long to be, with You in glory,
Prepared as a bride to receive her King.

Cleansed in Your holiness,
Clothed in Your righteousness,
Forgiven and glorious,
Washed in Your love.

Chapter 1

Here Comes the Bride

"I will keep myself looking beautiful. I will cook whatever meal you want as often as you want. I will do the dishes, clean the house, and do the laundry with a smile on my face; but listen, don't you ever try to hug me. I don't like that mushy stuff. Don't hug me." No fellow I know would want to be married to someone like that.

Neither does Jesus.

Unfortunately, His Church has far too often been just such a Bride. We have been very good at doing things for Him. We gladly give and serve. We are constantly going on missions trips, attending conferences, and being involved in an endless variety of wonderful programs. Christians tend to be very, very busy people.

All the busyness may seem fine, but there is a better way. I believe that God is calling His Church to be passionately in love with Him. Mark 12:30 says that we are to love the Lord our God with all our heart and soul, mind, and strength; in other words, with everything we have. That is how we are to love Him. It is only *then* that we can do our "housework" with the right motivation. You are probably familiar with the story of Martha and Mary found in Luke 10:38-42. Each of us has a daily choice as to which one of these sisters we will be like:

> As Jesus and His disciples were on their way, He came to a village where a woman named Martha opened her home to Him. She had a sister called Mary, who sat at the Lord's feet listening to what He said. But Martha was distracted by all the preparations that had to be made. She came to Him and asked, "Lord, don't You care that my sister has left me to do the work by myself? Tell her to help me!" "Martha, Martha," the Lord answered, "you are worried and upset about many things, but only one thing is needed. Mary has chosen what is better, and it will not be taken away from her."

Worship is the highest calling and first priority of the Church. I had previously understood that the highest call and first priority of the Church was to go and preach the gospel to all nations. But then I began to imagine what it would be like to have a group of people out there preaching the gospel who are radically in love with Jesus. I think our efforts would be much more effective, don't you?

One of the wonderful things that I have seen within the context of the renewal here in Toronto is that God is doing a work in our hearts. He is causing our hearts to really believe that He loves us. He wants a motivation that says, "Father, thank You for loving me. Thank You for the way You first demonstrated that love by sending Jesus to die for me. And, Father, because of the love which You have breathed into my heart, it is my delight to serve You. It is my joy."

Motivation is the issue. When our motivation is correct, we have much more energy. Yet we don't want to be in a position where we busily do stuff for God in order to get "brownie points." The same principle is very true in the area of worship. We don't worship God because we think He'll love us more. We don't even do it because we think He'll like it. We do it because He is worthy.

I have discovered, much to my amazement, that worship is really not a hard thing. As a matter of fact, I have noticed that children often worship better than we adults do. Why? Because worship is easier rather than harder. Did you know that mountains, hills, trees, and rocks are capable of worshiping God?

> *You will go out in joy and be led forth in peace; the mountains and hills will burst into song before you, and all the trees of the field will clap their hands* (Isaiah 55:12).

> *"I tell you," He replied, "if they keep quiet, the stones will cry out"* (Luke 19:40).

If rocks can do this, there is hope for us!

Most of us have a deep longing to draw close to God—to get to know Him in a more intimate way. However, there may be roadblocks along the way that keep us from getting to the place we long for. Some people may enter intimacy with God quite easily, but most of us struggle in this area. We come into worship times with the hope that somehow we can touch the Spirit of God, but often come away feeling that we missed something. And on the rare occasions that we perhaps feel the wonderful closeness of His presence, we are stirred with a longing for more.

Our relationship with God is spiritual. In intimacy, our spirit becomes one with the Spirit of our God.

> *That all of them may be one, Father, just as You are in Me and I am in You. May they also be in Us so that the world may believe that You have sent Me. I have given them the glory that You gave Me, that they may be one as We are one* (John 17:21-22).

We can become one with God. In fact, First Corinthians 2:10-13 says that we can actually know and understand God's thoughts as His Spirit reveals them to us!

> *...God has revealed it to us by His Spirit. The Spirit searches all things, even the deep things of God. For who among men knows the thoughts of a man except the man's spirit within him? In the same way no one knows the thoughts of God except the Spirit of God. We have not received the spirit of the world but the Spirit who is from God, that we may understand what God has freely given us. This is what we speak, not in words taught us by human wisdom but in words taught by the Spirit, expressing spiritual truths in spiritual words.*

Intimacy with God means to come into the closeness of His presence. It is entering into the Holy of Holies. In worship we can choose to remain in the outer court, on the fringe, and not really enter in. God wants us to step into the inner court, where, through the sacrifice of Jesus, we can be washed and cleansed from sin and self and be drawn into a close relationship with Him. And He is calling us to enter even further—into the Holy of Holies, the inner chamber of His glorious presence.

Many of us have had glimpses of this place, but Jesus tore the veil so that we can enter into His presence at any time (see Mk. 15:38).

> *Therefore, brothers, since we have confidence to enter the Most Holy Place by the blood of Jesus, by a new and living way opened for us through the curtain...let us draw near with a sincere heart in full assurance of faith...* (Hebrews 10:19-20,22).

The Lord wants us to come into His presence not just to visit, but to remain. He desires, as Acts 17:28 states, for us to actually live and move and have our very being in Him. He wants us to be continually in His presence. Sadly, many of God's people don't even realize that this kind of relationship with Him is possible. I used to be such a person.

In 1987, I received a phone call from a man whom I had never met. His name was John Arnott. He said, "Jeremy, I'm a pastor, and I think that God is calling me to plant a church in Toronto. We want to do this by having a weekend seminar first. I understand that you have some PA equipment. Could we use it for free?" *Interesting approach*, I thought, but I agreed to provide the equipment as long as I was the one to run it. (I didn't want anyone else messing with my gear.)

I set it up at the appropriate time, and a guy walked out and began to sing the most intimate love songs to Jesus I had ever heard. They went right into my heart, breaking me. I had never before seen a person just being so vulnerable before the Lord. I found myself wondering, *God, what is this? What kind of intimacy is this? I've got to know more about this.*

When the worship was finished, another guy walked up and gave a message. However, it wasn't a three-point sermon. Now you must understand that I was convinced there were right ways and wrong ways to preach, and as far as I was concerned, a three-point sermon was the only right way. This was no three-point sermon, but as I listened, I found myself thinking, *This is okay*. It was like, "Come sit in my living room, and let's talk." It was okay.

After the man finished speaking, the group went into what was called "body ministry." I had never heard of body ministry before. I had never seen body ministry before. He said, "I want the ministry team to get up and begin to walk up and down the aisles and just begin to pray for whomever you see the Holy Spirit resting on."

At this point, my seminary training kicked in big time, and my antennae extended fully. I was standing back at the soundboard with fear ripping through my heart. *They are weird. I am in the midst of weirdness, and these people walking down the aisle are getting closer to me.* So I began to get busy on the board. What I was trying to do was send out signals: *Don't talk to me. I'm very busy right now.* But no PA system was being used. No one was talking into a microphone. It was completely quiet. But there I was at the soundboard being busy—very busy. *Don't talk to me. Surely you can see that I'm very involved with something of utmost importance right now.* Nobody came near me. I was the most relieved person in the world when that meeting was over. The worship had been wonderful, but the ministry was just more than I could handle.

So I went home, and the next day being Sunday, I went to my church. My church was the safest church in the world. You arrived, and the service started at 11:00. And I don't mean at 11:01; I mean 11:00. We began with a hymn. It was the same hymn every week, year in and year out. You can't get any safer than that. I loved it. Words of welcome and a brief prayer were followed by a very polished music group. Then we would sing a hymn together, three verses, not four—three verses. After the offering came a three-point sermon. It was done right. We had a three-point sermon and an altar call. At 12 noon on the dot it was over. Nobody's dinner ever got burnt in the oven. You knew exactly when you would get home—always. It was perfect. I loved it. It was me.

Well that day, when we got to the part where we sang the hymn, I decided to do something I had picked up from being at the seminar the day before. As the hymn began, I thought, *I'm going to give this to You, God.* I had never done that before. For me it was always more a feeling of, *Let's just get this done. Come on, let's sing it and get it over with. Good, it's a short hymn.* Now, here I was saying, *I'm going to give this to You, God.* To my utter amazement, as we got toward the end of the first stanza, the same presence of the Lord that I had felt the day before was there. It was there in *my* church! I was completely surprised and delighted.

When we finished the first stanza, the gentleman who was leading worship said, "Stop! For the second stanza I want you to sing with all the gusto you've got!" He often did things like that, but it had never bothered me until then. Now his voice shook me out of where I had been with the Lord. I took a deep breath. *Okay. I'm going to focus in again on You, Jesus. I'm going to sing this just for You.* And again He was there. That sweet presence of my Savior was there.

Now I knew that the song leader was going to stop us again between verses because he usually did. But I thought, *I'm not going to let it shake me this time. I'm going to stay focused, and then through the third verse, it's You and me, Jesus. It's all ours.* Sure enough, at the end of the second stanza the song leader said, "Stop." *No problem, I'm focused.* Then he said, "For the third and final stanza, I want just the ladies to sing." My heart dropped. The sense of disappointment was so strong that I recognized I had been wrecked for worship. God had won my heart for intimacy.

Just so you know, I still love that church very much, and we visit it once in a while. I have wonderful friends who are still there, and the Lord is definitely at work in their midst. But I just found that God had so captured me that I had to find that place of intimacy with Him, specifically in the area of worship.

I long to worship You, my God,
to be intimate with You
in the secret place.

Ezekiel 44:15 says "...the priests...are to come near to Me to minister before Me...." Please understand that this is God speaking, and that in the New Covenant, the New Testament, you and I are now the priests. First Peter 2, verses 5 and 9, tell us that we are a priesthood of believers. That makes us right up there with guys like Samuel. I don't know how you feel, but I feel just a tad inadequate when it comes to ministering to God. How on earth can I minister to God? I can choose to love Him, I can choose to serve and obey Him, I can choose to worship Him—and somehow this ministers to Him.

Indeed, we have the ability to touch the heart of the One who created everything that has ever been created. And not only do we have the ability to do this, but He's asking us to come and do it. There is an open door.

When you open your heart to someone's love, you are placing yourself in a position of vulnerability. You are taking the risk of being hurt. Imagine! The God of the universe is actually choosing to be vulnerable to us.

Listen, humanity's track record has generally not been very good. If I were God, my response would probably be to close up my heart and get defensive and bitter. But God doesn't seem to do that. He seems to keep His heart open and to ask us to come, knowing that we will probably let Him down. He just keeps saying, "Come and touch My heart. It is open before you." What a God He is to become that vulnerable to us. Amazing. He wants a close, intimate relationship with us.

> *Why would You, the God of the universe,*
> *be vulnerable to me?*

Throughout Scripture, our relationship to God is compared to that of marriage. We are called the Bride of Christ. I believe that God established marriage for the purpose of giving us an example of oneness with Him. In a good marriage, there is a oneness, a meeting of spirit to spirit. Marriages these days are often so fractured that we are losing the effectiveness of that example. In fact, I believe that the reason satan is attacking marriages so severely is to destroy the beautiful model that God gave of His intimate love for us.

God is calling us into a romance with Him. He wants us to look into His eyes that are filled with love. Did you know that His eyes never leave us (Ps. 34:15), and that He wants us to fix our eyes upon Him (Ps. 141:8)?

When you look intently and longingly into the eyes of someone you love, you meet deeply with that person—spirit to spirit. You can send messages of love to one another without a word being spoken. It has been said that the eyes are the windows of the soul. (Have you ever noticed how some people avoid looking into your eyes? It is because a connection takes place when people look eye-to-eye, and they are avoiding getting close to you.)

Think about it: When you want to be intimate with someone, you want to be in a nice, quiet place where the two of you can share deeply with each other, isn't that right? In that atmosphere there is a gentleness, a peace, and a sweetness. Connie's definition for intimacy with God is this: It is the ability to run into the Father's arms (even when we've been bad). It is being able to sit on His lap, look into His eyes, and revel in His love. It is the capacity to let His love soak into you freely. It is also the ability to remain there, not just visit.

I run to You, my Father.
Hold me close in Your embrace.

When I am seeking to draw close to God in worship, I find it helpful to picture Him in front of me. Then I try to look Him in the eyes and sing my songs of love directly to Him.

We must make a conscious choice to press in to a deeper relationship with Him; and He is faithful to respond to our longing. In fact, that kind of longing is something He is constantly searching for. It is none other than His gift to us.

There is a transparency involved in drawing close to God. To be intimate with any person, we have to choose to become vulnerable and genuine. The more we choose to share with another person, the closer we become to him or her.

In Psalm 139 there is a wonderful example of David expressing his transparency before God. He acknowledges that God is intimately acquainted with all his ways. Then he bares his heart to God, asking Him to search his heart in order to reveal any wicked way in him and to lead him in everlasting ways (see Ps. 139:23-24). David was so confident of God's love for him that he was able to trust Him completely with his heart. When we are convinced of God's incredible and unconditional love for us, we, like David, can give God permission to search our thoughts and reveal what is inside our hearts.

When we consider that one of the main reasons we were created was to enjoy fellowship with God and worship Him forever, it is understandable that one of the enemy's greatest goals is to keep us from that intimacy with God. There is a spiritual battle going on as the enemy seeks to separate us from the Lord. But when we press through and enter that intimate place, we realize that the effort is worthwhile.

What Prevents Us From Intimacy? Fear

Sometimes we don't want to look God in the eye and allow Him to search our hearts because we ourselves don't want to acknowledge what is really inside us. Many of us have a poor self-image and don't want to take the risk of vulnerability. Laying our souls bare before God can be a frightening concept if we have the view that God will be harsh with us; but when we have an understanding of His unconditional love, we realize that He can be trusted. Perfect love will cast out and get rid of the fear in our hearts (see 1 Jn. 4:18).

What Prevents Us From Intimacy? Sin

First John 1:6 tells us that if we walk in the darkness, we cannot have fellowship with God. If we justify our sins instead of admitting them, we are deceiving ourselves. Sin separates us from God. Again, we need to understand God's love for us. Whenever He reveals sin or wrong attitudes in our lives, it is only because those things separate us from Him. His constant desire is to cleanse us and bring us into a closer relationship with Him (see 1 Jn. 1:9).

What Prevents Us From Intimacy? Discouragement

Life beats us up. In Psalm 42, David speaks to his own soul. He asks (KJV), "Why are you cast down? Why are you disquieted within me? Hope in God!" We need to command our own souls to start trusting God. It is a choice. We can choose to trust Him. We can also choose to praise Him—even when we don't feel like it. This is our "sacrifice of praise," as seen in Hebrews 13:15. And as we choose to put on the garments of praise, that spirit of heaviness falls aside!

What Prevents Us From Intimacy? Distractions

Earning money, raising kids, taking care of our home, serving the Lord in some area of ministry...we need to do all these things, but they are not to be the focus of our life. If they are our focus, we see everything else through them, including God. The remedy for this is to "seek His face" to make a connection with the Lord. As He becomes our focus, we will see the issues and responsibilities of life in clear perspective.

It is amazing how quickly we get distracted from Him, even in a worship service. We may be watching the worship team and evaluating how well they are singing or playing, or we may be looking around at our friends. Our minds wander off so easily, but as we turn our faces and our eyes toward Him, we can connect with Him and enter into that intimate place.

What Prevents Us From Intimacy? Wrong Theology

Many people are caught in the trap of religion. They are walking with God out of legalism, not relationship. Some don't realize that it is possible to hear God's voice. Others have not been taught that the Holy Spirit is still active and can work powerfully in our loves today. If you are such a person, ask God to reveal Himself to you, ask to see Him as He really is.

What Prevents Us From Intimacy? Hurts

If we have suffered many hurts in life, it is difficult to place ourselves in a vulnerable position, even with God. Many people have put up walls around their heart to protect themselves from being hurt again. The more we have been hurt, the bigger the walls have grown. Then, when we come before God in worship, we wonder why He seems so distant. Unfortunately, the walls we have built to keep people out also keep God out. If we can allow God to start melting those walls with His love, and if we choose to trust again, we will find ourselves with soft hearts toward God and others. Can we trust people not to hurt us again? No, we can't...and God doesn't promise that we won't be hurt. But He does promise to heal us, and as He heals us, He puts His protection around our hearts so that wounds don't penetrate so deeply.

The hurts we receive from family members, particularly our fathers, probably affect us the most. God created fathers for the purpose of loving, nurturing, and affirming us, and for giving direction for our lives.

In fact, He wanted fathers to represent Himself to us so that we could each know what our heavenly Father is like. When our earthly father fails us, we get a distorted picture of what God is like. If our father was harsh and critical, we tend to think that God will be harsh and critical with us. If our father wasn't available when we needed him, we have trouble trusting that God will be there for us. If we didn't have a close relationship with our father, we may have difficulty believing that God really wants to have a loving relationship with us.

God would like to redefine the word *Father* for us. He wants to be the father that our earthly fathers could not be. He wants to heal our wounded hearts with His incredible love so that we can now receive our nurture and affirmation from Him. He is the only One who can perfectly meet our need for love.

I need Your love, my Father, to set me free.

The pathway to being set free from the effects of the hurts in our lives is to walk in forgiveness. One of the hardest things in the world is to forgive a father who has been emotionally, physically, or sexually abusive. It really is hard, but all God ever asks of you and of me is that we choose to forgive.

Your heart may be raging and saying that your father doesn't deserve to be forgiven...and the truth is that he probably doesn't. However, neither do we deserve to be forgiven by the Lord. We may feel that there are many reasons not to forgive, but if we want to be healed, we have to be willing to let go. You see, it is our wrong responses to being hurt that hold us in bondage to those hurts. If we choose to forgive and to allow God to do His healing work in our hearts, we can be set free to respond in new ways.

The most wonderful effect of becoming more and more healed is that we enter into an intimacy with our loving heavenly Father that is deeper than we ever believed possible. When we come before Him to worship Him, we come with our hearts overflowing with thankfulness for all that He has done for us. When we reach out to Him, we can touch the heart of the Father in a deeper way. We can look into His eyes of love and let Him speak of His love for us. We can meet with Him spirit to Spirit and experience the fullness of worship.

Healing in our relationships with people is of great importance in the area of worship. Matthew 5:23-24 tells us to make things right with our brother (or sister) before we try to offer anything up to God. I suspect that this includes our offerings of song. (We will deal more thoroughly with the subject of forgiveness in Chapter 5.)

The biblical analogy of bride and bridegroom depicts a romantic relationship between God and ourselves. Jesus, the lover of our souls, has been actively pursuing us. He wants us to respond by passionately pursuing Him. Our desire for Him should cause us to make overtures toward Him! First John 4:19 says that we love Him because He first loved us. As we do our part and pursue Him, God will again respond.

Consider the example of Moses. He was 80 years of age when he first stood before the Egyptian pharaoh. During his time with the children of Israel in the desert, Moses climbed Mount Sinai a number of times in search of the Lord. It took effort for his old legs to climb that mountain! Moses pressed into the Lord with a diligent heart, and God met with him there (see Ex. 19:3-4). If we are to receive anything from God, we need to press in to Him. Then He is faithful to meet us. Jeremiah 29:13 promises that we will find the Lord when we search for Him with all our heart.

John 4:23-24 are verses that many of us know quite well.

> *Yet a time is coming and has now come when the true worshipers will worship the Father in spirit and truth, for they are the kind of worshipers the Father seeks. God is spirit and His worshipers must worship in spirit and in truth.*

God is actively looking for worshipers. It is something that He does a lot—24 hours a day, 7 days a week, century in and century out. He is continuously looking for people who will love Him. He is not necessarily looking for people who are busily doing things for Him. In fact, Matthew 7:22-23 tells us that many people will someday stand before Him, listing off all the things that they accomplished for Him, and the Lord will say, "Depart from Me. I never *knew* you...I never had intimate fellowship with you."

Scary thought, isn't it? Imagine serving God with intensity your whole life and then being greeted with that statement. Now you might be asking, "But how?

How can I reach that place of intimacy with God? How can I get closer to Him?" Listen, if that indeed is your heart cry, God is faithful. My suspicion is that instead of struggling to attain that intimacy, you may actually need to be in a place of letting go. There is a place for Christians that is a place of rest.

What a dichotomy this is! On the one hand, I'm telling you to press in wholeheartedly, and on the other hand, I'm telling you to let go and relax! The key here is the kind of effort we are to extend. Hebrews 4:11 tells us that the striving we are to do is to strive to enter into His rest. This is the kind of work that we are to be involved in, and out of that place will come the effortless flow of His ministry through us. There is a place where we can just abide. That's where I want to be. I want to live in a place of rest and abiding.

Jesus, draw me into Your rest.

Listen, even Jesus didn't do everything. He didn't heal everyone. He certainly could have, but Jesus was very good at hearing His heavenly Father and doing just what the Father asked Him to do. One example to consider is the Acts chapter 3 account of a crippled beggar outside the temple gate called Beautiful. Jesus must have passed that man many times and never healed him. It wasn't until after Jesus had died, was resurrected, and had gone to Heaven that Peter walked up to that cripple and said, "Silver and gold I do not have, but what I do have I give you: In the name of Jesus Christ of Nazareth, rise up and walk" (Acts 3:6

NKJV). The man jumped up praising God. Jesus could have healed that cripple long before that day, but the Father had a different plan.

In a similar manner, you don't have to do everything. You just have to do what God tells you to do. And where will you hear His voice? You will hear Him in the place of rest.

As we open ourselves to God, He shows us how precious we are to Him. He pours healing into our hearts and assures us that we are loved just for who we are, not because of what we do. We are loved just because we are His son or daughter. He longs to speak this into the depths of our being in a way that our hearts can understand.

One of the things that has absolutely amazed us in Toronto is the number of pastors and pastors' wives who have come here feeling completely burned out. They have had it. They are tired of phone calls at three in the morning. They are tired of being yelled at and criticized for doing the best job they know how to do. Christian leaders by the hundreds have come to Toronto Airport Christian Fellowship for times of healing and refreshing. There is a longing in their hearts to get back to the reason why they went into ministry in the first place, back to their love for Jesus.

If you are feeling tired and burned out, may I encourage you to listen to the voice of the Father and do only those things He tells you to do? May I encourage you to fall passionately in love with Jesus and let the power of His love energize and bring life to your acts of service for Him?

Right now, wherever you are, will you find that intimate place with Jesus? Will you pause in all the busyness of your life, quiet your soul, and make your heart open, surrendered, and vulnerable to Him? Will you say, "Yes, Lord." Will you allow Him to love you?

Father, I pray for the precious people who are reading these words. I pray especially for every weary believer; every Christian who is tired of striving; every member of Your Bride who has been caught up doing and serving instead of simply loving You. Father, I ask that You will come and meet with these persons right now. Let them feel Your presence and let them soak in the river of Your acceptance, forgiveness, and unconditional love. Light a new fire of passion toward You within their hearts.

Lord, we are so thankful that You love us...You really, really do....

We've reached the end of this first chapter, entitled "Here Comes the Bride." In most books, you would have carried right on into Chapter 2, but I encouraged you to do something a little different.

I would again like to suggest that you close this book and take time right now for your audience of One. He's the only reason for my writing or your reading. Stop, quiet your soul before Him, and wait for Him to meet you...now, today.

The Father Really Loves You

(Jeremy & Connie Sinnott)

The Father loves you.
The Father loves you.
The Father loves you.
He really, really loves you!

You really love me. (You really love me.)
You really love me. (You really love me.)
You really love me. (You really love me.)
You really, really love me!

Cause my heart to believe, that You could really love me.
How I need Your healing touch. Teach my heart
to receive....when it's hard to believe.

I really love You. (I really love You.)
I really love You. (I really love You.)
I really love You. (I really love You.)
I really, really love You.

In my brokenness I need You, to be a Father to me.
To nurture and protect me, to be a safe place for me....
Melt my heart, set me free.

Chapter 2

Voice of the Bridegroom

The Father loves you. He *really, really does.*

There is nothing more significant to the human race than being aware that our Creator loves us. Realizing the depth of His love may indeed be beyond our ability to understand; but comprehending even a fraction of that love will change us from within and breathe life into our very being. We cannot grasp how wide and long and deep and high the love of Christ is unless the power of the Holy Spirit reveals it to us (see Eph. 3:18-19). In these days, God has been pouring out His love in deeper ways than we could have ever imagined.

> *How great is the love the Father has lavished on us, that we should be called children of God!* (1 John 3:1a)

Too often we are like the man who stood before Jesus and said, "I believe." But with his very next breath he said, "Help me in my unbelief" (see Mk. 9:24). Our minds do believe that God loves us; we've read about His love in the Bible. Yet our hearts may not fully believe. *How could God love me?* we reason. *I know what I'm like. I know what a mess I am. I don't even like the way I am, so how could God love me?*

We may have trouble convincing our unbelieving hearts, but this is not a problem for the Lord. Ask Him! Certainly if He can change the hearts of pharaohs and kings, He can change our hearts as well.

In recent times, God seems determined to reveal His heart of love toward us. Sometimes His love has taken us by surprise! Shortly after renewal started here in Toronto in January 1994, a young man walked up to me and said, "Jeremy, while we were worshiping tonight God healed me." This fellow began to explain how he had gone to all kinds of chiropractors and doctors for his back and had been on all kinds of medication, and apparently nothing had worked. Every time he just bent over a little bit, there would be excruciating pain. I said to him, "You mean that during worship someone came up to you and said, 'in Jesus' name be healed,' or something like that?" And he said, "Nobody came up to me at all, but while we were worshiping, God healed me!" Then he bent over a couple of times and said, "See, there is no pain!"

And I blurted out some words that really showed where my heart was. I said to him, "You mean God did that all by Himself?!"

It wasn't more than a week after that when another fellow walked up to me after worship and said, "Jeremy, while we were worshiping, I became a Christian." And I said, "Did not." Now you need to understand that we had not talked about the four steps to peace with God during worship. We hadn't sung "Just as I Am" even once. We hadn't done anything evangelistic. So I asked him to tell me what had happened.

"While we were worshiping, it felt like Jesus was standing right there beside me, and yet I felt awful," he explained. "I felt dirty. I kept remembering all the stuff that I was involved in and all the stuff that I had done. Then I recalled my mother telling me when I was young how Jesus had died for us, that He had paid the price we should have paid for all the stuff we did wrong; and how He shed His blood on the cross for us. So I just told Jesus that I was sorry, and that I wanted to live for Him forever. I wanted to give Him my future—as long as He would stand that close beside me for the rest of my life."

I didn't say it out loud, but you know what I was thinking: *He did it all by Himself. Again.* Of course I knew that God was certainly capable to do it all by Himself. It was just that I had never seen Him do it like that. In my Christian experience I had been taught that we are God's hands, His feet, His mouthpiece—that God uses people to do His work. And now here He was doing it without us! There was a part of me that said, *This is great*, and another part that said, *Hey! That's **my** job!*

My church background had been one of structure and order, and I really appreciated that. I like things to be done very orderly and properly so that I know exactly what is going to happen next. I find great peace and security in knowing what the rules are. That's where I thrive. Just tell me what the rules are, and I will obey them and do my very best to not make any waves. Part of that stems from my 18 years as a school principal where orderliness, discipline, planning, and communication were high priorities.

Now here I was on staff at a church that just seemed to flow, and we had a pastor named John Arnott who was able to sense what God was up to and move with Him. It fascinated me. Both Connie and I were a tad bit nervous, but we trusted John. In fact, we felt right at home around him and his wife, Carol. They are two of the most loving people I know. Just being with them makes you feel protected. They don't put on any airs. They aren't one thing to some people and another thing to other people. What you see is who they are—all the time. There is no hype about John Arnott. When he preaches, the words just flow out from his heart in a "let's sit and talk here in my living room" kind of style. He has an outline, but John always remains wide open to whatever God is prompting him to say.

My seminary background caused me to value the hours of preparation that went into any particular message. However, the training I had received was a study-based preparation, whereas John's was more prayer and faith-based preparation. It's not that study isn't a priority to him; it's that he places a higher value upon prayer, hearing the Father's heart, and applying the Word of God. Being involved with something so wide open was a bit worrisome to me at first. I remember John making the comment, "I like a church that is just a little out of control." What he was referring to was a church that is a little out of man's control and a lot in God's hands. I thought to myself, *I believe that. I really like that. But in practical terms, I'm scared to death. I'm not used to this. I'm not sure if I trust this.*

Well, when renewal hit, things got more than a little out of our control. As pastors, we began to catch on that God was actually pretty good at doing things by Himself—over and over again. "How do we fit into all this?" we all wondered. The pastoral team began asking the Father for some words of direction, and He did give us some words. Actually, we thought He gave us two specific words: "Shut up." As you might realize, those are two very difficult words for pastors. What we were hearing God say went something like this: "You've had all your ducks in a row. The program is too organized, and there is little room for Me. Will you back off and give Me some space? Let Me do My work. Let Me speak to My people. They need to hear My voice, not yours."

Speak, Lord; I long to hear Your voice.

Now you need to understand that when I went to seminary I learned some important keys to running a church service. I learned that the last thing you ever want in your church program is silence. Any silence was a sure indicator that you had messed up and had totally lost control. *Yes, that's what we want to see—loss of control, humanly speaking, and relinquishing of control to the Holy Spirit.*

Since God was asking for some space, we felt that we had better give Him some. So we purposefully began to leave gaps in the meetings where absolutely nothing was happening.

Now it is one thing to be waiting in the midst of a congregation. There is no responsibility there. You can just wait. You can like it or not like it, but you don't have to do anything. It is quite another thing to be the one standing up there on the platform waiting and thinking, *God, it would be good if You would come now, and if You don't come, we are both going to look kind of stupid. You are probably not worried about that, but I am a little concerned about it.*

Somehow, we have this idea that if we have gaps of silence in a meeting we are wasting people's time. However, we are not wasting *God's* time, and He's the One we're concerned about, right? I like to compare moments of silence to the settings when many of us get the best ideas: We aren't thinking or doing a million things, the phone isn't ringing, and we are just alone and quiet—like in the bathtub, for instance. I've had the greatest ideas come to my mind as I've just laid there in the water and quietly soaked.

We began to discover that God loves to do things in the midst of silence, and He is pretty creative. In fact, we began to believe that maybe God could even run His own Church. Now this was a brand-new concept to me. Since when did God run His own Church? (Consider for a moment the state that the Church is in. Well, there you go.) Over the past number of years we have been observing that as we back off and get out of His way, God is very, very creative in how He orchestrates a meeting and how He ministers to people. He comes and heals people and brings deliverance easily and gently.

We are just beginning to experience a small part of what we believe the Lord wants to do in His Church. We are expecting an even greater presence of the Lord. John Arnott says, "Evangelism used to be when you knocked on doors. That was hard work. Then there was relational evangelism where you would casually talk to your friends and neighbors about the Lord. Now, we are moving into 'presence evangelism' where you don't say a word." Thousands are coming to Jesus all over the world every day. They are hearing His voice, the voice of the Bridegroom, and they are responding.

When it came to my role of being the worship leader, I really struggled. Who am I to assume that I can hear God and therefore make a decision to say, "Okay, congregation, this is where we are going to go because this is what God wants right now." How could I lead without being manipulative? Most people don't realize how manipulative music can be to achieve a desired result.

God has been so faithful to me in this journey. He is gently drawing and wooing me and winning my heart over and over again, saying, "Jeremy, I'll take the congregation where I want them to go." I know well my inability to lead, to do everything just right, and to bless people, but I know that God can do it. So I'm learning. I'm learning the wonderful mixture of being His hands, feet, and mouthpiece and yet, at the same time, of letting God, who is very capable in the farthest extreme, do it all by Himself without my involvement. It is a wonderful daily exchange of how He wants me to function and how He wants to function. And gradually, my caution has given way to simply trusting Him.

I trust You, Holy Spirit, to move how and where You want to.

In the setting of leading worship, once we are into that quiet, intimate place with Him, I do and say very little. Any instructions I give are at the very beginning of the meeting because the moment I start to talk, the people's focus turns from the Lord to what I am saying. Many worship leaders, full of good intentions, may actually pull people away from worship by trying to lead them into it. So I'm very careful to give any instruction at the beginning and then simply allow the worship to flow. If there comes a point in the meeting where I'm not sensing His direction and I don't know what to do next, I don't do anything. I do nothing. That is probably the hardest thing to do, but it is usually exactly what God is asking.

This approach is intimidating to a worship leader. After all, isn't it a leader's job to instruct and guide and lead? Isn't that the expectation of the pastor and the congregation? What freedom there is in just worshiping Him—worshiping before an audience of One. If you happen to be a worship leader, the very best way you can lead people into worship is for you yourself to worship. Worship. Don't talk about it, do it! Go into that intimate place; enter the Most Holy Place yourself, and the congregation will be drawn into that same place. Sing and play your instrument for Him, not for the people, and you will more than likely find the people right in there with you.

Father, I speak a blessing right now over worship leaders and worship teams. I speak a blessing of rest and say to these worshipers, "You don't need to make it happen. You don't need to make anything happen."

Father, I ask that Your wonderful Spirit would just flow gently as they take their positions on stage and stand before the congregation. I ask that You would breathe the breath of life; let streams of living water flow gently through them. And, as they stand in that position of rest, sometimes saying nothing, sometimes speaking or singing, Father, let them lean hard on You. Let them find that place of rest. Let them perform only for You, their audience of One. Amen.

I remember the day when someone first told me that worship should be a two-way experience. This was quite a shock to me. I had always thought that worship was a one-way experience: I gave my love and adoration to God. I realized then that I hadn't been coming with the expectation that God would speak to me or minister to my heart in times of worship. But the truth is, God longs to tells us how much He loves us.

The voice of joy, and the voice of gladness, the voice of the bridegroom, and the voice of the bride... (Jeremiah 33:11 KJV).

Do you hear the voice of the Bridegroom on a regular, daily, moment-by-moment basis? One of the scariest verses I've ever come across is John 10:27 (KJV): "My sheep hear My voice...." I must have read that at least 50 times over the years, but one day, as I was entering a new place in the Lord, I looked at it with my eyes open. *I don't hear Your voice. Aren't I Your sheep?!* Fear gripped me and I couldn't move from there. *After all these years, don't You know me? I don't hear Your voice. Aren't I Your sheep?*

I want to give you some keys that really helped me to learn to hear God's voice. They are part of a teaching by Mark and Patti Virkler.[1]

Habakkuk 2:1 says:

I will stand at my watch and station myself on the ramparts; I will look to see what He will say to me....

Let's break it down a bit. To "stand at my watch [guard post]" means that we are to still ourselves in the presence of the Lord. We are just going to stand there, sit there, or lie there; we are going to be very still. There it is again—God's instruction to go to that still, quiet place where it is so much easier to hear His voice.

To "keep watch" means that we are to expect Him to speak to us. Keep watch; look for His coming; learn to recognize His voice speaking. This is an inward kind of watching. God speaks His thoughts through His

---

1.   See Mark and Patti Virkler, *Communion With God* (Shippensburg, PA: Destiny Image Publishers, 1990), 5,127ff.

Spirit into our hearts because, as believers, He dwells within us. I have been asked if this isn't the same thing that New Agers do. No, this is not the same because there is one big difference: New Agers listen for any voice. Good or bad, any voice at all will do. I, on the other hand, am very particular. I don't want to listen to anything from the enemy. I want to hear the voice of the Lord God Almighty, and His voice only.

I've learned to believe that God is able to speak to me and that His desire to communicate with me is much greater than the enemy's desire to deceive me. In a song my friend Rob Critchley wrote, he expressed our belief in a great big God and a little bitty devil. Sure, the devil has power, but God is a zillion times bigger! Luke 11:10-13 tells us that when we ask God for the Holy Spirit, He's not going to give us a stone, and He's not going to give us a scorpion. Exercise faith in God's Word. Ask Him to speak; then trust Him!

Speak, Lord. In silence I wait to recognize and hear Your voice.

God wants us to hear His voice and to speak to our fellow believers the words we receive from Him. This is known as prophetic ministry. What exactly is prophetic ministry? We have this idea that it's future telling. Sometimes it is, but generally the prophetic ministry means to speak encouraging words under the Lord's prompting and direction.

But everyone who prophesies speaks to men for their strengthening, encouragement and comfort (1 Corinthians 14:3).

Prophetic ministry is always to edify or, as John Arnott would say, "To build up, lift up, and cheer up!" We have some guidelines at our church in terms of prophetic ministry: no direction, no correction; no dates, no mates. For instance, we don't allow people to declare, "Thus saith the Lord, 'Stop disobeying Me! Quit your job and move to the jungles of Borneo.' " Oh, put a sock in it...unless, of course, you are recognized and released as having the office of prophet. God can speak to that person all by Himself. Back out of the picture. Let the Lord do that kind of telling. If you are feeling that you know God's direction for someone, pray it through. Talk to God and He will talk to the person. Prophetic words should confirm what God has already been telling a person. Far too many people have been hurt by directional "prophecies" and by heavy-handed, manipulative, condemning words that are spoken under the guise of being a prophecy.

There is a big difference between <u>conviction</u> and <u>condemnation.</u> Condemnation brings death. That's from the enemy. Romans 8:1 tells us that, for the Christian, there is no condemnation. When we mess up—and we do—the Holy Spirit will draw it to our attention. Romans 2:4 says that it is the kindness of God that leads us to repentance. Condemnation makes us feel lousy and like giving up. It is very vague and we may not even know what the problem really is. It has the mark of the enemy all over it. But when the Holy Spirit brings correction, it is with life and hope. Such correction is also specific so that we can take specific action.

Prophetic words are always to be redemptive in nature. There are only a few people in our setting who have the freedom to give correctional words. We know these folk and their track record. We also know that any word of correction will be given with a sense of hope: There will be light in it and it will be ministered lovingly and with mercy. It will be spoken from a desire to comfort and restore people.

Teach me, my Father,
when and how to speak what I hear from You.

Joel 2:28 tells us that God will pour out His Spirit and that people will see visions, and sons and daughters will prophesy. I believe that God is raising up a prophetic generation, a generation of Christians who will speak forth His word with clarity. We are hungry for that. Christians worldwide have an intense hunger for the reality of His presence. We are tired of "playing church," of going through the same religious motions for an hour or two every Sunday morning. We long to hear His voice. We want to hear the songs of Heaven and to sing those songs out in the midst of the congregation. I believe that we will, but learning to do this is a process.

I vividly remember the first time I ever sang a prophetic song. We had received some teaching on the prophetic, and I thought that it would be a good idea to just step right out and try it. There were about 400 people in the service. What a way to start. I opened my mouth and sang. Well, it wasn't heresy, but it was what I would call "barely biblical." I put the guitar down, and as I walked off the stage I was thinking, *Jeremy, that was so stupid. You are a fool. How could you do that?* Guess whose voice I was hearing at that point...and I was wholeheartedly agreeing with him.

When I sat down, I saw John Arnott walking toward me. I thought: *This is my last day here. I'm fired. Well, I'll just tell him not to worry; it will never happen again.* But John said, "Jeremy, keep going for it." I looked at him in shock. *Were you listening? Did you hear what I said?* "Keep going for it."

I want you to know in all honesty that if he had said anything but that, it really would have been my delight to never again attempt to sing a prophetic song. I would have told myself, *I am not called to this. It is for other people.* But I don't believe that at all. I believe that it is for everybody—sons and daughters. We are a prophetic generation in both song and the spoken word. But it's a process and we are still learning.

Let me give you an analogy. Imagine a dad with his one-year-old son. One afternoon the father calls out, "Honey, get out the camera! Set it up. I think he's going to walk! Today's the day!" So the camera is rolling and Dad puts his son up on his feet. "Okay. Come to Dad!" And you know what happens. The little guy has his hands up in the air. Then he takes a faltering step and, wham! Down he goes on his little bottom. Now can you imagine that dad saying, "He fell! I can't believe he fell! He will never walk. He's just not called to walk"? Of course he wouldn't say that. Instead, he will pick up his son and put him back on his feet. Then the boy will take another faltering step or two and fall down again. It's a process, but after awhile he learns to walk. Most of you are walking okay. Some of you are even running.

Everyone I know who moves in the prophetic has stumbled a little bit. Now, I'm not talking about the future-telling type prophecy we see in the Old Testament. That has to be 100 percent accurate or it just isn't God. This falls into moving in the office of a prophet. There are very few of those guys around. What I'm talking about is the edification side, the speaking words from the Father's heart that build up, lift up, and cheer up. We are all called to do this.

Home groups are a wonderful place to exercise this. In such a setting you can step out and try, and still be loved if you mess up. I know people who now run in the prophetic, but they started out stumbling and walking slowly—and they still stumble occasionally. It's a process.

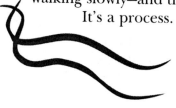

Let's take another look at Habakkuk chapter 2. Verse 2 (NAS) says to "record the vision." Write down what God speaks to you. Remember it. Many people are learning how to hear God's voice. They pray, ask God a question, stay quiet for a few moments, and then simply write down what they hear. This process is often called journaling.

A young man named Benji once journaled,

" 'Why does Dad always get so mad all the time?'

Benji, I'm bringing you through many tests right now. And I'm teaching you and him many things. You are now going into spiritual adulthood and you must learn many things. Your dad and mom will get stricter on you for a short time, and during this time I will teach you many things. Some of your friends will dislike you because you are getting wiser and more spiritual. I love you and your parents love you, and I will be interceding for you at the right hand of the Father during this time.

'Lord, will You help me have a better attitude towards my elders and my school work?

Yes! All you have to do is ask for My help.

'Please help me to have a better attitude!'

OK. But first I want you to yield yourself to Me and allow Me to take control.

'I want You to take all control over me and I yield myself to You.'

Benji, you will have a better attitude all the time. You are very very special to Me. Thank you for yielding to Me!

'I love You very much.'

I love you, too, Benji.[2]

Now, as you read this, was there anything in it that violates the Word of God? If there is anything in the voice we hear that contradicts or violates the Scriptures, it's not God's voice. It is as simple as that. There is light and life in what Benji wrote. I think that he

---

2.   Taken from Mark and Patti Virkler, *Communion With God*, 123.

heard the voice of the Lord. God's desire is that we all hear His voice.

Father, I ask Your Holy Spirit to minister to all Your children who just read these pages. Many of them have been listening to Your voice for years, and this is nothing new to them; but to others, this is very new. Lord, we want to choose to believe that Your ability to respond to us is far greater than the enemy's ability to deceive. I ask You to protect us from his voice. Father, we want to hear Your voice, the voice of the Bridegroom. Lead us on in this process. Lead us on in the wonderful journey of knowing You. Amen.

Now, once again, I encourage you to close this book. Quiet your heart and ask the Lord a question. Listen for His voice. He wants to speak to you...all by Himself. There are two questions that I recommend, which I know God loves to respond to: *How much do You love me?* and *What areas of my life do You still want me to surrender to You?* As you ask these questions, be sure to also pray, "As You speak to my heart, help me to say, 'Yes, Lord'."

I'll Say Yes

(Jeremy Sinnott)

If You will lead the way - I'll say yes, Lord.
If You will search out my heart - I'll say, yes.
If You will send me out - I'll say yes, Lord.
If You will show me the way - I'll say yes.

I'll say yes to You, Lord.
I'll say yes, yes to You, Lord.
I'll say yes to You, Lord.
Lord, I'll say yes.

If You will ask me for more - I'll say, yes Lord.
If You will ask me for my life - I'll say, yes.
If You will ask me for my heart - I'll say, yes Lord.
If You will ask me for it all - I'll say, yes.

Chapter 3

Voice of the Bride

The voice of joy, and the voice of gladness, the voice of the bridegroom, and the voice of the bride, the voice of them that shall say, Praise the Lord of hosts: for the Lord is good; for His mercy endureth for ever: and of them that shall bring the sacrifice of praise into the house of the Lord. For I will cause to return the captivity of the land, as at the first, saith the Lord (Jeremiah 33:11 KJV).

One of the most amazing things that has impacted me personally in the area of worship began at a Bob Fitts concert. Bob's wife, Kathy, was on stage with him, and as I watched her, I was drawn into worship. She was just going for it, worshiping with all her heart. Afterward I got a chance to talk to Bob, and I commented to him, "I noticed that your wife didn't have a microphone." He smiled and answered, "She can't sing." (Since then, Bob has told me that Kathy actually sings quite well.)

I thought, *God, You're telling me something here. I was drawn into worship by some girl who can't sing a note. You are telling me something.* And what He was saying to me was this: "I don't care how well a person sings. I'm the One who gives people their voices, after all. What I want to know is where the person's heart is." And her heart was right where He wanted it to be—just going for it.

I thought, *Okay, it works for Bob, but will it work for me?* When I got back home I began a quest for the worst singer in our church, and I found her. It wasn't even hard. I just noticed some people standing around her when she was singing and saw their expressions. (Just so you understand, I talked to this lady and got her permission to tell you this story. She said that it would be okay.)

This woman's name is Carol Arnott. She is our senior pastor's wife. Trust me, she cannot sing, but can that lady worship! So I went up to her and said (and I knew that I needed to do this very carefully), "Carol, I'm doing a little experiment, and I wonder if you would help me." I wanted a commitment before I told her what I was going to do. She said, "Yes." Then I continued, "Carol, I'd like to have you join the worship team next week."

Her face went white; then she laughed. Then she stopped laughing as she realized that I was serious. I explained what I wanted to do, and although she was not real keen about it, she had already committed herself.

We got together with the soundman and the three of us agreed to have her microphone turned off. She was happy; I was happy; the soundman was happy. Everybody was happy. And it turned out to be one of the most intimate times of worship I can ever remember. It was true. The heart of the worshiper was the key to what was happening. It was the key to our Lord's response within worship.

I love John Wimber's definition of worship: "It is a personal and intimate meeting with God in which we praise, magnify, and glorify Him for His person and actions. It is the act of freely giving love to God. We meet God, and He meets us."

There are many ways in which we can express our worship, but in this book we are primarily dealing with the area of our song. There are about 85 places in Scripture where we are encouraged to sing our praises before the Lord. If you read Psalm 47:6, you will notice that this verse tells us four times to sing our praises to Him. I know that some of you might be saying, "Jeremy, you don't understand. If I ever actually began to sing out in worship, it would end worship. It would finish worship. I can't sing on pitch. I have the worst voice in the world. People run away when I begin to sing, so I've learned to not sing at all, to lip sync, or to whisper."

The presence of the Lord is not dictated to by excellence in music. Listen, I've checked out the Scriptures to see what God's Word says about song. To be honest, I was looking for verses that said stuff like, "When thou singest thine song, be surest to sing on pitch with a minimum of vibrato. When thou singest thine harmonies, be surest to sing in thirds and fifths, never sevenths." I was looking for those good practical kinds of things. There was nothing in that area. But do you know what I did find? Psalm 100:1 tells us to make "a joyful noise." I can do that; you can do that; we all can do that...and without really caring what other people think about us. You see, worship is not for other people. Worship is for God.

> *Oh, my Father, I long to worship You—*
> *to feel the closeness of*
> *Your embrace, to smell the*
> *sweetness of Your breath,*
> *to hear the beating of Your heart.*

This is often a real test of where your heart is. If you find yourself being really worried about what other people think, you need to focus back onto your audience of One. You are a member of His Bride, and He longs to hear your voice lifted in praise to Him—both when you are alone and when you are in the midst of the congregation (see Ps. 68:26).

At the Toronto Airport Christian Fellowship, we are continually changing the musicians on our worship teams. If you really believe that the heart of the worshiper is the issue, most members of your congregation should be able to come up and sing on the platform. I've tried to help our people break out of an "I am in the audience" mentality into a realization that "I am part of the worship team." If you are a Christian, the universal quality of worship is, you are in.

So I began to watch the congregation, and whenever I noticed a person who was really worshiping, I would approach him or her. Now there are some people who are just not comfortable standing up front, and that's fine. I understand that. And there are some who can't stay on pitch, so again we would simply agree to turn off the microphone. I would tell them just to worship, to worship in exactly the same way they would worship in the congregation. If all of a sudden they were on the team and they began to dance around or be overly demonstrative, I would ask them, "Are you doing that because you feel an increase of God's presence or something? If you do, go for it. That's great. But if you are doing that just because you know you are being watched, stop. Just be who you are. Be who you were in the congregation. That's who I want you to be, because there will be people in the congregation who are just like you." After rotating large numbers of people on stage to be part of the platform ministry, the congregation got it. They really understood, "*We* are the worship team." God has called the Church to be a worshiping Bride.

These days, after having laid that foundation in the people's hearts, we do have regular worship teams. With the multitude of services, plus the conferences and teaching sessions, it is just so much better to minister alongside a group of people who are used to working together. Some of our musicians are on staff in some capacity. Others are part of our volunteer program. We have two different worship leaders and a large number of vocalists who are on a rotating schedule. By doing this, we have been able to meet for rehearsal and prayer on a regular basis, and hopefully, we are starting to reach a higher level, both musically and spiritually.

When choosing members of the team, I look for a wide variety of worshipers. I look for people to minister from the platform who are comfortable in raising their hands, but I also want people up there with me who don't raise their hands. Demonstrating different types of worship will help a greater number of people to enter in. I want people to feel comfortable so that we can concentrate more on the issues of the heart than on what we may be doing on the outside or how good our voices are.

We all come in different packages. By that I mean different denominations and different styles of worship. There is a measure of beauty in the diversity of these packages. It is my opinion that God loves all the packages. The beauty of denominations is that you get to worship in the way that is you. Some of us are quiet, and there are places around that worship in a quiet manner. Some of us are real loud and rowdy, so there are places you can go where the people are loud and rowdy in their worship. The issue is not so much whether one package is right and another is wrong, or one is better and another is worse. God loves them all. The issue is that no matter which package we come from, the focus must be on where our heart is and where our one-on-one relationship with our heavenly Father is.

I know that the people who walk in through the doors of our church buildings will fit somewhere between two extremes. On the one hand, some people who come have been very fortunate. God has blessed them at every turn, and everything they have done has been turning to gold. So they come in and sing their songs of thanksgiving. But on the other hand, I also know that there are people coming in whose lives are a wreck. Their marriage is falling apart, their kids are in rebellion, they have just found out that they have terminal cancer, and on and on and on. For them worship is truly a *sacrifice* of praise. That is to say, worship is work. It is hard for them to do it. But we invite and encourage them to choose to worship just because God is worthy.

Whether we sing a song of thanksgiving or a sacrifice of praise, God is still worthy of it. Do you know that a sacrifice of praise is just as acceptable in His sight as a song of thanksgiving? It is so amazing as we sing and worship, how God responds and begins to bring healing. I have often watched those individuals whose lives are total wrecks; as they begin to choose to worship and enter in, some of their burden is just removed. God begins to do a work in their hearts.

> *I choose to worship You, Lord Jesus, no matter what the circumstances of my life may be. Accept my worship and move in my heart.*

Within my few words of instruction at the very beginning of worship, I try to set people at ease. I encourage them to worship in whatever way they feel comfortable. Some people don't want to lift their hands. They don't want to dance. They don't even really want to stand up. They just want to sit quietly and be close to the Lord. And I say to them, "If that's you, please do that. Be yourself. Be comfortable." At the same time, however, we ask them not to judge or be irritated by those who are dancing, clapping, running, or shouting. There are some people who are quiet, and some who are rowdy. I think we can allow plenty of room for both, and we need to appreciate each other's differences. <u>The beauty of the Body of Christ is in our diversity.</u> We need each other to be who He has created us to be. Some are feet; others are hands, noses, or eyes. Some worship quietly. Others worship loudly or go into groaning intercession as soon as they sense His presence. My suspicion is that God's ability to receive worship encompasses the loudest of the loud to the quietest of the quiet—even silence. God can be worshiped in absolute silence. He is just wide open for worship.

> *Help me, Lord Jesus, to worship You*
> *in the way that is right for me, and not to*
> *judge other people because their worship style*
> *is different from mine.*

I appreciate the influence that the Vineyard has had upon our congregation. One aspect of this influence has been the freedom we have to come to church casually dressed, not needing to wear suits and ties and such things, but clothes that are comfortable. We believe that it is actually okay to sit, or even to lie, on the floor. Some people even bring a pillow and blanket and just lie down in His presence; others might leap freely with shouts of laughter...and it's all okay. This is to say that folks generally find an atmosphere of both freedom and safety around our church, and that's good.

Our goal is that nothing is done for effect or to manipulate either God or the people. I know as a worship leader that there are certain things I can say or do that will affect the congregation. It is not a hard thing to simply say, "Let's do this" and "Let's do this," and to get a frenzy going fairly easily. But, ultimately, I want the Lord to do any manipulation that is done. I want Him to be the Manipulator, and I want us to be the responders.

It gives me great joy when I see prophetic song or singing in tongues originate from the congregation. I place high value on this because it is probably God breathed, and it is not a situation where the worship team is performing. We are in this together. So we want to listen together, to see what God will do, and to respond to Him. We let Him be in control. It's healthy when He controls our worship, but it is unhealthy when I do it. So I want to back off more and allow Him to do it.

If a prophetic song comes from a member of the worship team, we want to be sensitive so that the congregation does not feel left out. We want them to be participants, not spectators. So, sometimes, as a song goes forth from the platform, we will gently nudge the people to respond to what is being sung. They might repeat each phrase or sing their own song. Or, we might say something like, "Why don't you tell the Lord how much you love Him right now and receive what He is saying through this song." After the prophetic song is over, we might play the instruments and ask the congregation to put their own words to the music. Then the whole congregation, even the little children, lift up "I love You's" to the Lord. We try to keep everyone involved. The Lord loves to hear the voice of His Bride responding to Him and loving Him. Often when a prophetic song is released, it takes us to a new level of worship as God speaks forth His heart.

There are three kinds of prophetic songs. In the first, God's heart is expressed to us through a spontaneous song. In the second, God's heart and perspective are expressed to us in a song prepared ahead of time. In the third, spontaneous songs are lifted to the Lord as an expression of our heart's response to Him. (See Ephesians 5:19.) This prophetic music, or singing new songs to the Lord, is very new to some people, so we need instruction and practice. We have been realizing the importance of training our worship teams, in particular, in this area. Although we practice flowing together as a team, the best place to practice this is when we have our own time with God. When we are alone with the Lord, we can practice expressing to Him what is on our hearts through spontaneous song, and we can practice listening to His voice and singing out loud what we have heard Him speak.

Lest you think that the Church has been discovering new territory in this area of prophetic song, please understand that King David did this all the time. He or another worship leader would sing a song prophetically over the congregation, and the congregation would, as one, give a prophetic response in return.

When God's presence falls upon a congregation and He expresses His heart to His people through prophetic music, it is a truly wonderful thing to behold. His glory seems to come down upon us, encompassing us in His love and His presence. It permeates the very depths of our being. His glory changes everything.

24-Hour Tabernacle Worship

<u>God loves to hear the voice of His Bride.</u> He loves it so much that He wants to hear it all the time. Perhaps this is why something that is often called "Tabernacle Worship" is happening in various places around the world. Numerous churches have been gathering musicians and worshipers together for periods of nonstop 24-hour worship. In fact, this continuous worship is becoming so common that we are asking the Lord if this is something that He is breathing out in a universal manner across the globe.

Tabernacle Worship is nothing new. It is old stuff...real old stuff. David did this all the time. It was his thing. Worship in David's tabernacle was nonstop. In a sense we are just rediscovering what has been. The tabernacle represents one of the most incredible times throughout the history of the Bible because God's glory and His presence were resident there. He was with His people all the time. I want to find such a place where I am constantly residing in God's presence. Right now, I feel that I am just visiting, but I want to get to a place where I am abiding with God. I want to remain in His presence.

I long to live in Your presence, oh God, every moment of every day.

Let's take a sweeping, overall look at the biblical pattern of Tabernacle Worship. Be forewarned that we will be getting into some names and numbers, but please stay with me so that you can get a picture of what this was actually like. It was incredible!

All the Levites who were musicians—Asaph, Heman, Jeduthun and their sons and relatives—stood on the east side of the altar, dressed in fine linen and playing cymbals, harps and lyres. They were accompanied by 120 priests sounding trumpets. The trumpeters and singers joined in unison, as with one voice, to give praise and thanks to the Lord. Accompanied by trumpets, cymbals and other instruments, they raised their voices in praise to the Lord and sang: "He is good; His love endures forever." Then the temple of the Lord was filled with a cloud, and the priests could not perform their service because of the cloud, for the glory of the Lord filled the temple of God (2 Chronicles 5:12-14).

One hundred and twenty priests were blowing trumpets. In my whole life I never heard more than seven trumpets playing in unison. I have heard more than that playing different parts, but I have heard only seven trumpets being played in unison—and it was awesome. It was also loud. I can't imagine what 120 trumpets would sound like.

Then God's Word goes on to say that the singers joined with the trumpets in unison. There was a unison thing that was happening here. They were all singing or playing the same part. The singers were all singing the same words, specifically, "He is good, His love endures forever."

These are the men David put in charge of the music in the house of the Lord after the ark came to rest there. They ministered with music before the tabernacle, the Tent of Meeting, until Solomon built the temple of the Lord in

Jerusalem. They performed their duties according to the regulations laid down for them (1 Chronicles 6:31-32).

He [Solomon] stationed the Levites in the temple of the Lord with cymbals, harps and lyres in the way prescribed by David and Gad the king's seer and Nathan the prophet; this was commanded by the Lord through His prophets (2 Chronicles 29:25).

My point is that God directed all this. He directed it through the prophets. It was a God-breathed idea. It was His idea. That is why it worked. David established what Tabernacle Worship was to look like, and David's son Solomon actually built the temple, but the whole idea came from God.

Three prophets headed up the original tabernacle worship. King David, who is referred to as a prophet in Acts 2:30 and Matthew 22:43, was in charge. Then there was Nathan the prophet (see 1 Chron. 29:29; 2 Sam. 7; 1 Kings 1:10-22). There was also a fellow by the name of Gad who was called a seer or a prophet (see 1 Chron. 29:29; 1 Sam. 22:5). An additional leader was a fellow by the name of Chenaniah, who was the chief of the Levites in charge of singing (see 1 Chron. 15:22,27).

Are you still with me? Picture this: Under the three prophets and the leader in charge of singing were more musicians and singers. These included Asaph, Heman, and Jeduthun (possibly also known as Ethan), who were directly under the supervision of King David (see 1 Chron. 15:19; 25:6). They were to sing and play bronze cymbals, together with the 14 musicians named in First Chronicles 15:20-21, who were to sing and play lyres and harps. First Chronicles 25 further names these

Levitical musicians, stating that "some of the sons of Asaph, Heman and Jeduthun [were set apart] for the ministry of prophesying, accompanied by harps, lyres and cymbals" (1 Chron. 25:1). These sons, 24 in number, together with some of their sons and relatives, totaled 288 (see 1 Chron. 15:19-21; 25:2-31). If we look at the span of a week and divide it up into segments, that's not bad. Huge worship teams could have been responsible for half a day. No sweat. But it goes on.

Do you know how many were in the orchestra? Read about this in First Chronicles 23:5, where it says that 4,000 musicians were to praise the Lord with musical instruments. I like it! You could give each of these guys two minutes and they could be done for the week. That's it. No problem! In First Chronicles 15:16, David told the leaders of the Levites to appoint their brothers as singers to sing joyful songs accompanied by musical instruments, lyres, harps, and cymbals. Oh, God likes joyful songs! As we enter into our Tabernacle Worship, that needs to be a component. I believe that there is a time to be serious and a time to be filled with awe. There is a time to bring reverence to the Lord and a time for joy. There is also a time for dancing.

Now please understand! The moment we talk about dancing as a form of worship, some people get offended. David had that problem. (See Second Samuel 6:16-22.) One day you and I are going to meet David, and I know that the first thing I'm going to ask him is, "How angry was your wife really?" Was it an 8 out of 10? Or was it a 15 out of 10? All I know is that she was really ticked. She was quite offended by the way David danced before the Lord. But David's response was, "I will be even more undignified than this!" His heart was just sold out for the Lord, and he knew where he was going. He knew what God had called him to.

First Chronicles 25:1 tells us that "David, together with the commanders of the army, set apart some of the sons of Asaph, Heman, and Jedethun for the ministry of prophesying, accompanied by harps, lyres, and cymbals...." The prophetic is a component of Tabernacle Worship.

> ...Then the temple of the Lord was filled with a cloud, and the priests could not perform their service because of the cloud, for the glory of the Lord filled the temple of God (2 Chronicles 5:13-14).

Whew! We made it through the names and numbers. The end result was that God liked it. He liked it so much that He moved right in, glory and all! I want to know what it is like not to be able to minister because His presence is so thick. I really want that. I want to hear what the song of the angels is like.

You know, in eternity that is going to be our experience. Right now, our vision is through a veil. We see through a glass darkly. There is coming a time, however, when we will see Him not just in our mind's eye, but face to face (see 1 Cor. 13:12). Then our joy will be to fall down and worship Him for eternity. This will be the joy of our lives.

 At our church, although we don't have the luxury of as many musicians and vocalists as in the first tabernacle, we decided to give nonstop worship a try anyway.

In the very beginning we thought, *Why not just play music 24 hours straight?*

So we just let the CD player run for 24 hours. We even got a 12-disc CD player and set it on random play so that it would choose different songs. But we discovered that the Holy Spirit knows the difference between CDs and live music. He likes CDs, don't get me wrong, and there can be a real anointing on recorded music; but He seems to like the real thing better. He seems to like the heart that is brought forth as people worship. Okay, Lord. Live worship it is.

Then we divided the time into two-hour segments and asked musicians to sign up for a time that was convenient for them. Some time slots were filled by worship teams and others by individual worshipers. It is one thing to have continual worship from 9 in the morning until 11 at night. It is quite another when it is 4 in the morning. I was really concerned about who would want to take those wee-hour shifts. To my amazement, those slots were the first to be chosen. There was a keenness to be involved.

I asked each leader who signed up to take full responsibility for his or her particular time slot. This meant that all were to organize their own worship teams, involving people they felt comfortable working with. They were free to use as many or as few musicians as they wanted. It was wide open. They were to feel free to sing in tongues, sing prophetically, shout, speak, and read the Scriptures. They could stand, kneel, clap, or just play an instrument. I told them that there might be times within the worship when silence would be appropriate. I asked them to use a variety of songs: from deep worship to songs of joy; both fast songs and slow songs. And above all, I emphasized that they were to have fun. "Enjoy this. You are not going to fail. Enjoy it!"

While we are having fun, we also need to be reminded of the warning Jesus gave to the Pharisees in Matthew 15:8: "These people honor Me with their lips, but their hearts are far from Me." It is very important that we worship from our hearts, and I feel that this is an especially important factor in Tabernacle Worship. This is not a performance. This is not entertainment. It is worship. Period. As soloists or worship teams in the Church, too often our approach has been, "We lead people into worship."

Tabernacle Worship has nothing to do with leading people. This realization forced a very healthy paradigm shift for many of our vocalists and musicians. We are not doing this to minister to people. Certainly, the people will be blessed by the presence of the Lord, but that is merely a by-product; it is not our goal. Although we invite the congregation to join us, this is not for them. Tabernacle Worship is not horizontal; it is vertical. It is an offering for our audience of One.

Lord Jesus, accept the offering of my hands and my heart lifted in worship to you.

When we started Tabernacle Worship, we did invite the congregation. I had expected to see people there throughout the day, but I thought that the crowd would be pretty sparse at night.

To my surprise, the lowest attendance we ever reached was 50. There were some people who stayed in the sanctuary all day and all night. They brought pillows and sleeping bags, and when they got tired, they just found a corner and went to sleep. Then they would wake up and get involved again.

The fact that you just keep on worshiping has, in itself, many challenges, many wonders, that I personally am becoming more and more committed to. I like how it tastes; I like what I see so far; and I enjoy seeing the fruit of what it is doing in the midst of our congregation. We started off with one 24-hour period. The last one we did was three 24-hour days in a row. The next one we do will be a seven-day, 24-hours-a-day Tabernacle Worship.

When we did Tabernacle Worship for a period of three days, we invited other churches to get involved. It was a grand thing having their participation because they brought a flavor of worship that was really different from ours. We had everything from choirs to one person playing a keyboard, and it all had a wonderful sense of flowing together.

 What are the reports we are hearing from the congregation? They are falling in love with Jesus all over again. In the past, I had some people who would come up to me regularly and say, "I wish worship wouldn't stop. It just gets going and it ends." Now those folks are absolutely delighted. "This is the best worship time I have ever had in my life. When is the next one?!" Our church is screaming for another Tabernacle experience. I am

really quite surprised by that. I thought that they would become tired of it. I thought that three days would wear them out, but they are crying for more.

Now the big question for me is, "Father, do You like it?" We've prayed, and this seems to be what the Lord is asking from us. So we are going to go for a seven-day Tabernacle Worship the next time. We're going for it not just because it seems like a good idea, but because we think this is the direction God is giving us. My expectation is that significant things will happen in the church as we worship. Psalm 22:3 (KJV) tells us that God inhabits the praises of His people.

We are still way behind the biblical precedent of worship in the house of the Lord; and yet we are approaching the days when I believe that we will hear the voice of the Bridegroom and the voice of the corporate Bride in our meetings. I believe that the day is coming when we will go to church services not to meet with each other and to learn about the Lord, but to know Him, to actually meet with Him face to face. What a wonderful time it is to be alive!

Father, we want to see You. We long for You like thirsty souls in a dry, parched land. We want Your presence...we want to abide in Your presence; to be with You not just to visit, but to remain there. We want to lift our voices in a new song of praise to You. We want to say, "Yes, Lord!"

You desire to hear the voice of Your Bride. Father, teach us to sing, to speak, and to pray in ways that touch Your heart. Teach us how to worship You. Teach us how to celebrate Your presence! Amen.

Get Ready

(Jeremy Sinnott)

Get ready! Get ready—oh come and let us sing,
Get ready! Get ready—oh come and worship Him.

There's the sound of marching,
I hear marching in the trees.
The Lord's gone out before us,
'Move quickly', is decreed.

The angels are responding
To the Captain of the hosts,
Our King is Jesus!
One with the Father and Holy Ghost. (3x)

Get ready! Get ready—come pray and intercede;
Get ready! Get ready—God surely will succeed.

The first line of battle,
Will be those who worship You.
We break down strongholds,
As we give praise to Him who's true.

We give You honour,
We praise Your holy Name.
Fill us with passion;
Come set our hearts a-flame. (3x)

Get ready! Get ready—the wedding is at hand;
Get ready! Get ready—for the wedding of the Lamb.

Chapter 4

Modern-Day Levites

...Unto Him that loved us, and washed us from our sins in His own blood, and hath made us kings and priests unto God and His Father; to Him be glory and dominion for ever and ever. Amen (Revelation 1:5-6 KJV).

Since God established the tabernacle as a working model of how to approach Him, I want us to take a brief, but closer look at Levitical worship. What I am about to share with you is but a synopsis of what a whole book could easily be written about. The Bible is rich with God's instructions in the area of holiness in His worshipers. To be a singer or musician in the temple, the first priority was that you had to be from the tribe of Levi. If you were from any other tribe you could not be a musician in the temple, no matter how talented you were. Revelation 1:6 tells us that Jesus has made us to be kings and priests unto God. We are now Levites, full-time worshipers! Our lives are consecrated to the Lord. We should be in constant preparation for ushering in the presence of God.

Do we really take this as seriously as we should? Do we go through regular cleansing before the Lord to have all the garbage cleaned out of our hearts? Do we listen carefully to the Lord's prescribed way for ushering His presence into our meetings?

Search my heart, oh God.
Cleanse me from all my sin.

First Chronicles 15:16-21 explains how the musicians were appointed. Out of the group of Levites (those chosen and consecrated to God) they chose people who were gifted with musical ability. David then appointed the leaders of the Levites, and then those leaders selected musicians according to their abilities. Some were even chosen by top authorities in the army. First Chronicles 25:1 says,

> *David, together with the commanders of the army, set apart some of the sons of Asaph, Heman and Jeduthun for the ministry of prophesying, accompanied by harps, lyres and cymbals....*

In verses 6-7, it goes on to say,

> *All these men were under the supervision of their fathers for the music of the temple of the Lord, with cymbals, lyres and harps, for the ministry at the house of God. Asaph, Jeduthun and Heman were under the supervision of the king. Along with their relatives—all of them trained and skilled in music for the Lord—they numbered 288.*

The line of authority was clearly defined. David, the king, just happened to be a musician, but it was his kingly authority that was the important issue here. In other words, the leader of our congregation, namely the pastor, has authority over the worship ministry, regardless of whether or not he is a musician. Fathers were also mentioned as having authority, as the skills and training were passed down to the younger generations. It is important to value those who have gone before us and to learn from them. This prescribed pattern of authority also points out the importance of functioning as spiritual parents by mentoring the younger people under us.

It is also very interesting that the commanders of the army chose musicians. Again, these officers were probably not musicians themselves, but they had a position of authority over the musicians they chose.

What comes across strongly in these Scriptures from First Chronicles is that those who lead worship must be under authority and must respect those in authority over them, even in worship issues. This may seem to be difficult sometimes, because the pastor often doesn't understand music the way the worship team does. Nevertheless, pastors must have the authority to veto songs, request songs, or make decisions in regards to who or who is not on the team, since they are responsible for the overall ministry. When lines of authority are clearly marked out and respected—not just in obeying but also in honoring those in authority— many problems between worship teams and pastors would never happen. Let's recognize the pastor's position of authority over the army.

The worship leader is also a commander, although he or she is still under the authority of the pastor. This leader likewise has the right to make decisions that should be honored by the rest of the team. As with all those in positions of authority, the leaders should value and carefully weigh and consider the opinions of those under them, but the final say must be left in the hands of those to whom God has entrusted the responsibility.

The Ark of His Presence

... "No one but the Levites may carry the ark of God, because the Lord chose them to carry the ark of the Lord and to minister before Him forever" (1 Chronicles 15:2).

The Levites were responsible to carry the ark of the covenant, which was also called the ark of God's presence (see Ex. 25:22; Num. 7:89). When the Levites were carrying the ark, it symbolized that they were carrying the presence of God.

In First Chronicles 13, we read the story of when David wanted to bring the ark of the covenant into Jerusalem. Verse 7 tells us that the ark was brought from Abinadab's house on a new cart, with two men named Uzzah and Ahio guiding it. The Bible also tells us that David and the people were celebrating with cymbals, tambourines, and lyres. Their hearts were full of worship and their motives were right before God. However, a tragedy occurred:

When they came to the threshing floor of Kidon, Uzzah reached out his hand to steady the ark, because the oxen stumbled. The Lord's anger burned against Uzzah, and He struck him down, because he had put his hand on the ark. So he died there before the Lord (1 Chronicles 13:9-10).

It seems so unfair that God would do this. The people really wanted to honor God by bringing the ark into the city instead of neglecting it as before. If their motives were pure, why did God strike down Uzzah? It seems very logical that he should steady the ark if it was about to fall off the cart.

The answer to this question is found in First Chronicles chapter 15. David says in verse 13 that because the Levites were not the ones transporting the ark, the Lord broke out in anger.

God had given a prescribed way of carrying the ark: on poles on the shoulders of Levites; not on a cart. Exodus 25 and Numbers 4 give very precise details regarding the care of the ark and the other holy articles used in the tabernacle. Numbers 4:15 says that if they even touched the ark, they would die. The story of Uzzah shows that God keeps His Word.

David was angry because God had struck down Uzzah, but he was also afraid. So he took the ark aside to the house of Obed-Edom where it remained for the next three months, and the Lord blessed Obed-Edom's household as a result.

First Chronicles 15 tells how David tried to bring the ark to the city a second time. In verse 2, we see how he instructed that "no one but the Levites may carry the ark, because the Lord chose them to carry the ark and to minister before Him forever." This time David would not be careless; this time he did it according to the Lord's instructions. The Levites also consecrated themselves in preparation for carrying the ark.

The same issue still applies today. Things are to be done God's prescribed way, not the way we think they should be done. As present-day Levites, we are to inquire of the Lord every step of the way if we want the privilege of carrying His presence.

Show me, Lord, what You would have me to do.

Walk in Holiness

Scripture reveals that in the last days God's Spirit will be poured out, but His wrath will also come out against those who do not obey Him (see Joel 2–3). We are now in a time period when God's power is being released in a stronger way, and it has also become apparent that accountability for the use of that power is increasing. God has been cleansing His Church, which has resulted in the downfall of some Christian leaders. God will not continue to tolerate the sins of His people. Indeed, the time may well come when we will witness accounts similar to the story of Ananias and Sapphira in Acts 5:1-11.

Throughout the ages, but especially in recent times, the Lord has sent out a strong call that His people must walk in holiness and purity. The Levites were in a constant state of being cleansed. Every time they walked past the washbasin, the laver, which was in the center of the sanctuary, they had to wash themselves in it. In fact, they had to take off all their clothes, wash, and then put on clean clothes before they could walk any further. This was done every single time they walked by. It was symbolic of always being cleansed, of always being consecrated to God, of always being pure before Him.

> *I would be pure in my heart, my God. Reveal all that is impure and bring me to repentance.*

We have been realizing how important it is for us as a worship team, along with leaders in other areas, to really make sure that our hearts are being purified so that what comes out is pure. We are in a position of visibility and of awesome responsibility. People's hearts are very soft and vulnerable during worship. When music is played, the message goes first to the heart and then to the brain for processing. This is unlike a spoken message, which goes first to the brain and then to the heart. Since people's hearts are so open during worship, the anointing on our lives will have an impact on them. We want that impact to be positive. For this reason, it is very important that we continually let the Lord deal with issues in our heart and life, so that we may become holy vessels for His use; then the message that comes forth through us will be pure.

A Time of Consecration

That He might present it to Himself a glorious church, not having spot, or wrinkle, or any such thing; but that it should be holy and without blemish (Ephesians 5:27 KJV).

God is preparing His Bride. She will be passionately in love with Him. She will also be holy and pure. The Lord may be speaking to you right now concerning areas in your life or ministry where you have been doing things your way, not His. The Lord lovingly convicts us because He wants to purify us. He longs to take away the striving of our own efforts to accomplish righteousness and to give us His strength in our innermost being. Ephesians 3:16-17a says, "I pray that out of His glorious riches He may strengthen you with **power** through His Spirit in your inner being, so that Christ may dwell in your hearts through faith." He wants to break off bondages in our lives, take away sin patterns, and set us free! Only His power can do this; we are unable to do it ourselves.

I confess that I am in bondage to _____.
Work in my life, Lord Jesus, and set me free.

Throughout the world, Christians have been asking for the fire of God to come. Do we really know what we are asking when we ask for His fire? We are asking Him to purge and refine us. We are asking Him to burn out the dross, the sin in our lives, and bring us forth as pure gold (see Job 23:10; Zech. 13:9).

This is a time of consecration before the Lord—a time of being set apart as a worshiper, as a Levite to serve in the Lord's temple; and not just in the temple, but in our homes, our workplaces, our neighborhoods; indeed everywhere we go. It is a time for the consecration of our whole life as a sacrifice of worship to the Lord.

Father, we ask that right now You would come with consuming fire and burn up everything You don't want in our hearts. Set us on fire with passion for You. Thank You for the call You have given to each one of us to walk before You in holiness. Father, we want to surrender to You. We know that apart from the blood of Jesus we are guilty. Wash us afresh with that blood right now. Cleanse us, oh God. Every time we walk by that laver, cleanse us again. Every time a sinful situation occurs, like it does every day, wash us again. Every time we react wrongly to a hurt, please wash us again. May our lives be a pleasing sacrifice to You, and may we be faithful to carry Your presence everywhere we go.

First John 1:9 assures us that if we confess our sins, He is faithful and just to forgive us and to cleanse and purify us from all unrighteousness. We can then turn to a new chapter in our lives. We can rest in His strength and rely on the power of His Spirit to live in holiness and to worship Him as modern-day Levites—consecrated and set apart for Him; ready to take our places in the front lines of the spiritual battle that rages across the earth in these days.

Father Teach Us

(Jeremy & Connie Sinnott)

We will stand at the place
Of the Lord's threshing floor.
We will stand on the altar,
We pray You'll restore.

Give us eyes, give us ears
We are asking for more.
Let the watchman cry out,
Come call us to war.

Hear our cry oh Lord;
Hear our cry oh Lord;
Answer as we call Your name,
Hear our cry oh Lord.

Father teach us to intercede; teach us to go between.
Father teach us to mediate; teach us to represent.
Father teach us to reconcile; teach us to watch and pray.
Father teach us to claim victory; teach us to intercede.

Beyond words we may groan
As we pray out Your will.
We lay hold of the sword,
May Your plan be fulfilled.
In the name of the Lord
We do battle, we build.
The victory's won...
But the lost call to us still.

Hear our cry oh Lord;
Hear our cry oh Lord;
Answer as we call Your name,
Hear our cry oh Lord.

Chapter 5

Warrior Bride

Thou art beautiful, O my love, as Tirzah, comely as Jerusalem, terrible as an army with banners (Song of Songs 6:4 KJV).

God is raising up a Bride who is both tender in love and fiercesome in battle. He is calling forth a Church whose passion and love for Him strike terror in the heart of the enemy—a Bride wearing army boots. The Church has been weak and defenseless far too long simply because we have not recognized the authority that is ours in Christ; but in these days, He is empowering and releasing us. He is teaching us to stand firm against the schemes of the enemy through the authority of Christ in our lives. The Lord is building an end-time army. He is training and equipping us for spiritual battle. He is preparing us to bring in the great harvest. He wants to use us to set captives free and to loose prisoners from their chains as we bring them into His Kingdom of love (see Is. 58:6-7).

A Worshiping Bride

Worship has always been a significant element of spiritual warfare. As we worship, we are making declarations of God's sovereignty, which then releases things in the heavenly realms. We actually do warfare in the heavens as we declare His Lordship.

> *Let the high praises of God be in their* [our] *mouth, and a twoedged sword in their* [our] *hand; to execute vengeance upon the heathen, and punishments upon the people; to bind their kings with chains, and their nobles with fetters of iron; to execute upon them the judgment written: this honour have all His saints. Praise ye the Lord* (Psalm 149:6-9 KJV).

Please note that verse 9 says, "this honour have all His saints." Warfare through song is not for a select few; it is the honor and right of every believer—including you! In fact, even children do warfare as they worship. Psalm 8:2 tells us that from their mouths comes praise that silences the enemy! Their praise is powerful! The enemy cannot stand the presence of God; no wonder worship makes him flee!

*I praise You, my God.
Come and silence my enemies.*

Worshipers are called to be in the front lines of spiritual battle. In the Old Testament, the singers and musicians were placed in the front lines of battle. They went out ahead of the army, blasting their trumpets and worshiping. No doubt they were making declarations of God's sovereignty into the heavens, as well as on the earth. They were on the front lines in a spiritual battle that was being played out on a physical level. What a wonderful example of warfare through worship! Musicians would go ahead proclaiming God's Kingship, and as they lifted their voices, the Lord defeated their enemies. We can see this in the story in Joshua 6 where the worshipers went out in advance of the army, blowing their trumpets. On the seventh day, the walls of Jericho tumbled down as God won the victory for His people. There is much that the Church today can learn from the wars in the Old Testament. There is much that we can also learn from the lives of the people who fought in those battles.

Two Warriors—David and Saul

David and Saul were two individuals who were mighty warriors. Now it is interesting to notice that these two men both started out the same way. They were both very humble. In First Samuel 9:21 we can read Saul's reaction to his first meeting with Samuel. His initial response was, "Why do you say such a thing to me? I'm the least of my clan." And then, in First Samuel 10:21-22, when he was to be chosen as the first king of the nation of Israel, Saul couldn't be found. He was hiding in the baggage. Saul began in a good place, a place of humility.

In First Samuel 24:14, as David was being chased, he walked out one day and asked, "Why are you chasing a dead dog like me—a flea?" That's a pretty low opinion to have of oneself. Yet that's the kind of attitude God likes. Have you ever noticed that God doesn't choose the big guys? In fact, First Samuel 15:17 says, in effect, "when you [Saul] were little in your own eyes the Lord could use you."

I choose to humble myself before You, Father God.

Saul and David were both mighty warriors. In fact, the girls used to sing songs about them: "Saul has slain his thousands and David his tens of thousands" (1 Sam. 18:7). They were both anointed by Samuel and by the Holy Spirit. But, unfortunately, Saul's story took a wrong turn.

In First Samuel 13, we read an account of Saul in which he did not follow the plan he and the prophet Samuel had set. He had agreed with Samuel that the king and the people would go to Gilgal and wait seven days. At the end of the seven days Samuel would come, offer the sacrifice, and ask God what they should do; and Saul would do it. I love a plan.

So, Saul goes to Gilgal and he begins to wait. But, as he is waiting, he notices that the Philistines must be on the Internet or something. They have a great communication system, and they begin to show up in great numbers. The Bible says that they were as numerous as the sand on the seashore. If you ever want to waste some time on your holidays, pick up a handful of sand and count the grains. You won't make it to the end. You will give up; believe me, I've tried it! There are just too many of them. So here comes a Philistine army as numerous as sand on a seashore.

I've tried to identify with what Saul is going through in this passage. You see, warfare at that time was like a chess game—the object was to get the king. You might have some bishops, knights, and rooks to get through, but if you got the king, the game was over. Saul is the king, and he is a little more than mildly concerned. He is the enemy's target, and he has noticed that his army is getting smaller. His men are getting scared. They are starting to run away. Still he waits the seven days...but Samuel doesn't show up at the end of those days as he had said he would.

What would you do? I would probably do exactly what Saul did: *We're in this battle now. Let's just offer the sacrifice and get moving!* And the moment Saul goes ahead and does his own thing, Samuel shows up, and he doesn't have a good word. Do you know why? It was because not even the king could offer a sacrifice—only a priest could. Saul knew that. Saul directly disobeyed the command of the Lord by offering that sacrifice. And as a result, he lost his kingdom.

It is interesting to note that what happened was that Saul was looking with human eyes. He saw the huge army of Philistines, saw his own army getting smaller, and made a decision on the basis of human wisdom, not the Word of the Lord. As you read on in the life of Saul, you will see how step by step he moved further and further away from God until he didn't even want to hear what God had to say. And, ultimately, God withdrew from him. In the end Saul sought the advice of a witch, and the very next day he and his whole family died in battle. It really is a tragic ending for a man who started out the right way.

Forgive me, God. I too get tied in knots of
fear because I look with the eyes of my flesh.

But that was not the case with David. If you read the account in First Samuel 23:1-5,9-13, you will notice these words, "David inquired of the Lord." Over and over again you will read those same words. David sought his heavenly Father at every turn. Imagine, if you will, what it would have been like to be a soldier in David's army: "I've got my shield, I've got my sword, my boots are shined, and I'm feeling all right! We are ready for battle. Where is our leader? Where's David? *He's in that tent there.* What's he doing? *He's praying.* Praying is good. How long is he going to be in there? *Till he gets an answer.* We are going to stand here ready for battle until he gets an answer? Here he comes. He's got a smile on his face. We're going to do it." Then off they would go, and they would win the battle.

This became normal for David and his men. This happened all the time. "I've got my shield, I've got my sword, my boots are shined again, I'm feeling all right, and we are once again ready for battle; but where is our leader? Don't tell me. He's in that tent. He's praying. I knew that. And we are going to wait here till he gets an answer. Here he comes. He's got that smile on his face. We're going to do it."

And off they would go and win the battle again. What a system. I love it. Now, as we follow David's life in Scripture, we reach First Samuel 30:

David and his men reached Ziklag on the third day. Now the Amalekites had raided the Negev and Ziklag. They had attacked Ziklag and burned it, and had taken captive the women and all who were in it, both young and old. They killed none of them, but carried them off as they went on their way. When David and his men came to Ziklag, they found it destroyed by fire and their wives and sons and daughters taken captive. So David and his men wept aloud until they had no strength left to weep. David's two wives had been captured—Ahinoam of Jezreel and Abigail, the widow of Nabal of Carmel. David was greatly distressed because the men were talking of stoning him; each one was bitter in spirit because of his sons and daughters. But David found strength in the Lord his God (1 Samuel 30:1-6).

What's happened here? While David and his men were away, a group of Amalekites discovered their campsite, burned it to the ground, and took captive all the women and children. When David and his men returned, they were absolutely grief stricken. I was always amazed and could not understand why David's men were talking of stoning him. Why would they be so angry at David that they would want to kill him? Wouldn't their anger instead be directed toward the Amalekites? They were the ones who had burned the place to the ground and had taken the families; it wasn't David's fault. But look at this possible scenario: "I've got my shield, I've got my sword, my boots are filthy, and I am in a foul mood! My wife and kids are gone! We've got to get after them. Right now, we've got to get after them! Where's David? Don't tell me he's in that tent again. Get him out! What do you mean he won't come out? I'll get him out. I'll kill him!"

Let's understand, there is no police force here. Anything that is done, you do. Would you be standing around waiting a second if someone had stolen your family? I've got to tell you, far too often my heart is just like Saul's. I see with my eyes, and I respond on the basis of my own human wisdom. But I want a heart like David's.

Do you know what he was doing? He was in that tent asking God if they should pursue the Amalekites. God said "yes" to David, but that was not enough for David. He had to know more, so he asks God, "Will we overtake them?" Again God says, "Yes." So off they finally go and everyone is safely recovered. Everyone. What an amazing story!

David was waiting in that tent for his Father's answer. What a heart! Acts 13:22 says that David was a man after God's own heart. He had the heart of a worshiper. That's the kind of heart I want. That's where I want to go. I want God to change my heart, which is like Saul's, and give me a heart just like David's. In the midst of that kind of pressure and that kind of grief, in the midst of his own men talking of killing him, as well as his family being gone, what does David do? He turns to God. Prayer was a way of life for David. He knew that it was his greatest weapon.

An Interceding Bride

Throughout the world you can find pockets of people who are being called by God to fasting and prayer. It is virtually universal. God is calling the Church worldwide to a place of intercession. This is far more than the kind of intercession where we claim a verse and pray briefly over a person. It is more like a groan, like an inner cry that rises from one's spirit. It goes beyond words and often lasts for hours at a time as people "stand in the gap," as referred to in Ezekiel 22:30 (NKJV):

So I sought for a man among them who would make a wall, and stand in the gap before Me on behalf of the land, that I should not destroy it....

To *intercede* means "to go between, to stand between two particular individuals who are not seeing eye to eye." It means to mediate; to actively give words that soften each side; to be actually in the process of reconciling irreconcilable differences. Intercession also means to be a watchman on the wall:

Son of man, I have made you a watchman for the house of Israel; therefore hear a word from My mouth, and give them warning from Me (Ezekiel 3:17 NKJV).

Intercessors keep watch and then give warning, but the warning is always given to bring hope. Part of an intercessor's task is simply to proclaim the truth, which then brings the victory. In other words, intercession can be a declarative kind of thing, declaring Christ's victory and freedom for people. Please look at what Ephesians 6:10-13 (NKJV) says:

Finally, my brethren, be strong in the Lord and in the power of His might. Put on the whole armor of God, that you may be able to stand against the wiles of the devil. For we do not wrestle against flesh and blood, but against principalities, against powers, against the rulers of the darkness of this age, against spiritual hosts of wickedness in the heavenly places. Therefore take up the whole armor of God, that you may be able to withstand in the evil day, and having done all, to stand.

We are actually wrestling against spiritual forces. Intercession is real work. We are in a real war. Jesus has won the victory. Our job now is to declare it and see it established in people's lives. And this, again, is a process. It used to be that we would pray, and one in ten people would get healed. It was great for the one who got healed, but it was hard dealing with the other nine because they had good questions for which we really didn't have answers. Now I'd say it's more like five out of ten receive healing. We're growing as spiritual soldiers.

Intercession can be like childbirth. Romans 8:22-27 speaks about all creation groaning. Verse 26 says that we don't know what we should pray for, but the Spirit Himself intercedes for us with groans that words cannot express. Sometimes the Holy Spirit within us groans as we pray according to God's will. He is the one who empowers us to pray this way. In Galatians 4:19, Paul says that he travailed and labored in the pangs of childbirth until Christ was formed in the people to whom he was writing.

In all our wrestling and groaning, there is still a place of rest where we can live. The issue remains that we need to hear God's voice. That's where the answer is. Specifically as we look at the process of intercession, but also in terms of whatever we do, we need to hear His voice. We need to be cooperating with God, hearing the Voice of the Bridegroom, and praying out the things that He puts upon our hearts.

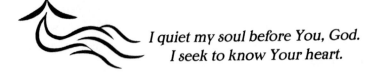

I quiet my soul before You, God.
I seek to know Your heart.

> *This is the confidence we have in approaching God: that*
> *if we ask anything according to His will, He hears us. And*
> *if we know that He hears us—whatever we ask—we know*
> *that we have what we asked of Him* (1 John 5:14-15).

As we listen to the voice of the Father, and as we
allow the Holy Spirit to empower our prayers, we can
be very effective warriors through our worship. Worship Intercession, as we call it, is using the powerful
vehicle of music to underscore prayer that expresses
that which is on the Father's heart. Sometimes during
a worship service the Lord leads us to pray along specific lines. As we flow with His Spirit, our voices and
instruments can become His prophetic tools to accomplish His purposes. There have been times when we
have set aside a meeting or a whole day where our only
agenda was to worship and pray as the Holy Spirit
instructed us.

Some of the deepest congregational intercession
has occurred as we have invited the congregation to
"stand in the gap" for an unsaved family member or
acquaintance, for our community, for our national
government leaders, etc. Often, as the congregation
begins to pray, the tempo and intensity of the continued instrumental music can serve to help guide and
direct the intercession. We need to be careful that we
don't manipulate the prayer through our worship, but
rather, the musicians need to respond to the ebb and
flow of the Spirit, making us facilitators of what the
Father wants to do. Sometimes the music may be tender, and the prayer will become soft and intimate.
Sometimes the drums are driving out a loud beat, and
the intercession becomes strong, with a bold cry of war.

*Teach me, Father, to pray in the
power and wisdom of the Spirit,
to pray what is on Your heart.*

Opportunity may be given for the intercessors or
the prophetic team to come up to a microphone and
give words of encouragement or prayer (which have
first been submitted to the pastoral team) while the
music continues. Scripture or a responsive reading
might also be given at this time. Or the Lord may give
someone a prophetic song, or a vocalist may begin to
sing a particular phrase over and over, with the congregation possibly singing that same phrase. Through
all this, a specific theme is often birthed; then the worship team often follows up on that by choosing an
appropriate song.

I love it when the whole congregation gets involved
in Worship Intercession. Sometimes the groanings go
beyond words. All, young and old, are able to con-
tribute and exercise their authority in Christ right
there in the midst of worship.

*Father, You are breathing into Your Church some-
thing that is brand-new, and yet, Lord, it comes down
to us from the dawn of time. You have always desired
to have those who would stand in the gap. Father,
You sent Your Son to do exactly that—to stand in the
gap and be our Intercessor. Thank You, Lord. And
Father, teach us. Teach us to pray and to worship You
in ways that do warfare in the heavenly realm. Train
our hands to war and our fingers to fight as Psalm*

144:1 tells us. As we clap our hands and play our instruments, do battle, Lord! Bring Your healing and deliverance! Let Your salvation come. Set captives free!

A Forgiving Bride

For us to really enter into our place as the Warrior Bride, we must experience deliverance in our own lives. Therefore we must ask ourselves, "What enemies are lurking within us? What unseen forces hold us back from experiencing real power and victory?"

Holy Spirit, reveal the obstacles
that prevent the breakdown of the enemy's
strongholds within my heart.

We have found that the greatest hindrance and obstacle to effective worship is unforgiveness. Does that surprise you? Forgiveness is so crucial, in fact, that we bring it up in every teaching session that we conduct. Even if we are speaking at a church for just one meeting, we will always bring up the topic of forgiveness. Psalm 66:18 (KJV) says, "If I regard iniquity in my heart, the Lord will not hear me."

Our relationships with other members of the Bride are very important; in fact, they are so important to the Lord that if we aren't right with people, He may not listen to us. We may lift our voice in Worship Intercession week after week, and we might do spiritual warfare with our songs...all to no avail. As Matthew 5:23-24 tells us, we must first be reconciled with our brother before bringing any offering to the Lord.

Each one of us has been hurt by somebody. When this happens, we basically say, "Ouch, I don't like that," and begin to build walls around our hearts. We build those walls for protection; we guard our hearts and begin to be very careful about what we let in. And it works. It works really well. The problem, of course, is that we also shut out the Lord by those walls.

Listen, it is far better to be vulnerable and allow ourselves to be hurt than to have a heart of stone. However, some of us have been wounded so deeply that it is very hard for us to break out of our walls. And what happens is that the moment we begin to judge people, we develop a hardness of heart.

Let me explain what happens in our human interactions. Someone comes along and kicks you in the shin for no reason. You didn't deserve it. As a good Christian, the first thing you do is appeal to God: "Father, I am an innocent victim of a brutal attack by that person. I demand justice. I appeal to You, my Redeemer and Protector, go get him!" And God responds with something like this: "Do you mean that you want Me to give him what he deserves?" "Yes," you respond heartily. "Well, I could do that," God says, "but, just so you know, I'll then have to give you what you deserve." You think for a moment, then say, "Let's review this, God. I'm the victim here. I did nothing. He was the one who kicked me. I want You to go get him!" And God very patiently explains, "If you want to work on the basis of justice for him, then you must also receive what is justice for you. If you want mercy for you, it must be mercy for him."

We can choose to live under the law, which works fairness—right and wrong, an eye for an eye—all that stuff. The law works, but the problem is that we can't keep it. James 2:10 tells us that the moment we break even the least of the commandments, we are guilty of all. That's a scary proposition. Do you want to live under the law and die? The only alternative is to live under mercy and grace.

I choose mercy, Lord Jesus.

Have you ever noticed how the enemy always operates on the basis of law? In deliverance ministry we love to say, "In Jesus' name, get out!" What if the demon's response is "no"? You might wonder what happened to your authority in Christ. It's still there, but sometimes the enemy has a legal right to stay—and often it is because of unforgiveness. If people live in unforgiveness, they are choosing the law; and because they themselves have failed in the law, the enemy has a legal right—he has access to them. So, when that legal point of entrance is dealt with, which again is often unforgiveness, then the persons can be set free from whatever it is that the enemy has put on them.

As I stated back in Chapter 1, a primary area of attack is the relationship between fathers and children. Many people say that they did not receive enough love and affirmation from their fathers, and far too many actually received some kind of injury from them instead. God wants to be your "Papa God," as seen in Romans 8:15. He wants to heal your heart and make you trust again. And He wants to help you forgive your earthly father and release him from your judgments.

Your receiving mercy and grace from the Lord is directly related to your own ability to flow in mercy and grace toward other people. The first step is that you choose to forgive, no matter what your heart says; then you ask God to deal with your heart. Trust Him. He is able to deal with your heart.

At this point, I want to invite you to take some first steps of forgiveness. You may have a list of a hundred people who have hurt you and with whom you are still angry. That's fine. I want you to choose one. Then you just apply the same principle to the other people on your list.

Father, we recognize that we are always in the process of becoming the strong and beautiful Bride that You are making us to be. Today, in the midst of our process and in the midst of our messing up, we ask that You would wash us. Father, we want no root of bitterness to rise up within us. We want no hard-heartedness or unforgiveness at all. We want to be free. We want to flow in mercy and grace. So, Lord, would You respond to the cry of our voice? Would You do that work in our hearts that we can't do?

Father, I ask now that You would place into each reader's mind the name of one person who has wounded and hurt him or her. One person, one situation at a time, Lord. Please help each to forgive. Amen.

Right here, right now, is an opportunity for you to deal with your unforgiveness and put an end to it! I invite you to read the following prayer out loud:

Dear heavenly Father, thank You for loving me. Thank You for forgiving me. I now choose to forgive [name the person]. *I choose to forgive him* [her] *for* [say what it is the person did to you; quietly list as many of the hurts that you can remember]. *I choose to release* [name the person] *from my judgments. I set him* [her] *free. He* [she] *no longer owes me anything; not even an apology. And heavenly Father, I ask You to forgive me for my wrong reactions* [list them] *and the way that I responded to* [the person's name] *and the way that I judged him* [her]. *In Jesus' name. Amen.*

Now by the authority that is given to me simply because I am a brother in the Lord, I pronounce you forgiven. I want you to receive that forgiveness because the enemy will come along and say, "Are you really forgiven?" You are. This day you are forgiven for those wrong reactions. First John 1:9 promises that if we confess our faults, He is faithful and just to forgive us. This day is a day that is set apart, and God will begin to breathe into you a new way of responding. If you feel the old judgments and reactions rising up within you, just repeat the three steps. Pray, "Lord, forgive me for judging again. I continue to choose to forgive (name the person), and I let it go." You can also learn to forgive as a way of life when people offend you on a daily basis. You will find that the sooner you forgive, the easier it is to let it go. When you have held on to resentments for a long time, it will take longer to walk out of old patterns. But now you have only the structure to deal with, not the grip or the hook of the enemy. And God will help you with that.

He will breathe a new heart into you. God specializes in dealing with the heart.

One of the most effective ways that God brings healing to a wounded heart is by revealing His perspective. Spend time asking Him to show you how He felt when you were wounded and see what thoughts come into your mind. Also, ask Him to show you the woundedness in the person who hurt you that would cause him or her to be hurtful to you. Let God pour His comfort and His healing love into your heart. Spend time resting in His presence.

You may have a list of 99 more people who have hurt you. I want you to get together with somebody who will pray through these steps with you. It is very important that you hear those words, "You are forgiven." It is also very important that you speak the words of forgiveness aloud.

Do you know that what is released on earth is released in Heaven? Take a look at Matthew 16:19. This is not just a physical thing; it is a spiritual principle. Before we can truly be a Warrior Bride, the Lord wants us to experience His victory in our own lives. He desires an openness in our hearts that allows Him to continually lead and teach us.

More Lord

(Jeremy Sinnott)

We cry more, Lord; more of You.
More of Jesus; fill us anew.

Give us more, Lord. Let it pour.
We choose life, Lord; more Lord, more.

Thank You Jesus,
for the privilege of Your presence.
Thank You Holy Spirit
for coming in power.
Thank You Father,
for Your mercy and endless love.

All power...is Yours!
All wealth...is Yours!
All wisdom...is Yours!
All strength...is Yours!
All honour...is Yours!
All glory...is Yours!
All praise...is Yours!
...is Yours!
...is Yours!
...is Yours!

Chapter 6

Human Beings—Not Human Doings

We are called "human beings," not "human doings." When I first heard that statement during a John and Paula Sandford seminar, it resonated in my heart. I have so appreciated their teaching in this area. Most of us have been locked into a "performance orientation" issue of doing and not being. Performance orientation is what we learned when we were about five years old.

We walked into the kitchen where Mom was doing the dishes, and we naively thought, *That looks like fun!* We picked up a cloth and a plate and put them together, and there was a startling reaction from our mothers that went something like this: "Thank you for doing those dishes! I love you so much!" We blinked a couple times and thought, *I like that.* So the next morning we got up out of bed, walked into the kitchen, grabbed the towel and plate, put them together, and were met with the same reaction. "I love you so much! Thank you for doing those dishes!" We thought, *I can live on this.*

But the next day we got up out of bed feeling grumpy, and we walked into the kitchen saying to ourselves, *I'm not doing the dishes.* We noticed that our mothers didn't tell us how much they loved us, and our five-year-old minds began to reason, *If you do stuff you get loved. If you don't do stuff, you don't get loved. If you do stuff, you have value and worth. If you don't do stuff, you don't have value or worth.*

Is there anything wrong with doing the dishes? No. Doing the dishes is good. It is the motivation behind doing the dishes that is the issue. You see, if a child does the dishes because it is the only way he or she knows that Mother loves him [her], that child is in trouble. We as parents need to tell our children how much we love them, even when they mess up or don't meet our expectations.

Well, here we are all grown up, and we have put childish things behind us...or have we? Childhood reasonings become life's foundation stones. Here's a personal example. When I hear a sermon on witnessing and evangelism, there is a process that I go through every single time: "Lord, Your Word says that You love me. That's good. But I don't witness enough, and You are probably not very happy with me about that. As a matter of fact, I was probably supposed to talk about You to that guy I met this morning, but I didn't. I was in a hurry. Lord, I know that You are probably very unhappy with me right now. You probably hate me, don't You?"

You see, my head knows that God loves me, but my heart hasn't fully believed. Now, evangelism and witnessing are important. We are all called to do that. The issue I'm dealing with here, however, is motivation. If I witness and evangelize because I think that this is the only way I can make God love me, I'm in trouble.

Reveal the wrong motivations in my heart, Lord.

Perhaps you are one of the many people who think: *I don't sing very well, and I don't speak publicly. I really don't have a lot of gifting in much of anything. If I'm compared to a part of the Body of Christ, I'm probably the toe. I'm probably the little toe in the Body of Christ. I'm probably the toenail of the little toe in the Body of Christ, and my favorite song is "Amazing Grace"—how sweet the sound that saved a wretch like me. That's what I am—a wretch. Nothing. Nobody. I have never done anything. I will never do anything. I'm gonna go out in the garden and eat worms.*

If you are in that kind of position, perfect! You're in exactly the kind of position where God will use you! I checked it out: God doesn't use proud people. He always goes for the outcasts, the poor, the lowly, the wretched. He even used some guy with a speech impediment to talk to Pharaoh to get the nation of Israel out of Egypt. Moses was described as the meekest man on the face of the earth (see Num. 12:3). You would have thought that God would get a leader with some pizzazz. But, no. He chose a meek man.

God loves to use people who can't do it. Why? Because those people know that *He can*! Look at what First Corinthians 1:26-29 (KJV) says:

> *For ye see your calling, brethren, how that not many wise men after the flesh, not many mighty, not many noble, are called: But God hath chosen the foolish things of the world to confound the wise; and God hath chosen the weak things of the world to confound the things which are mighty; and base things of the world, and things which are despised, hath God chosen, yea, and things which are not, to bring to nought things that are: That no flesh should glory in His presence.*

You are in a good place when your position is, "I can't do very much, but God can." But if you are continually trying to measure up to someone's expectations, or you are trying to make someone pleased with you, you will get very, very tired. Perhaps that is where you find yourself right now.

> *Father, I want to pray for those people who have been hurt by the negative, limiting words that have been spoken over them. I pray for people who are so tired of trying to measure up to someone else's expectations. Father, we want to freely admit that we don't measure up. Not one of us measures up. We are all sinners. We all fall short of Your glory. Thanks be to God—we have a Savior who is able to set us free despite our failings. Your love will never fail. You are the same yesterday, today, forever; and we put our trust and confidence in You.*

> *I just speak to people's hearts right now, and in Jesus' name I say: You are loved. You are accepted. It is not by your own might or your own power or your own*

*strength; it is the Spirit of the Lord within you who will accomplish the task ahead. He is able...and He lives within you. I speak rest to every weary soul. Cease from your own labors and strivings. It is **God** who works in you both to will and to **do** His good purpose. He will give you both the desire and the **ability** to do the things He calls you to do. Relax, in Jesus' Name.*

But the Lord said to Samuel, "Do not consider his appearance or his height, for I have rejected him. The Lord does not look at the things man looks at. Man looks at the outward appearance, but the Lord looks at the heart" (1 Samuel 16:7).

We need to get a whole lot better at seeing people the way God does, and quit being so concerned with outward appearances. Take worship teams, for instance. What the Church has typically been used to is a polished group of musicians coming out and, in a sense, performing for a congregation, who is, in a sense, the audience. I'm so thankful that many churches are moving away from this spectator mentality. More and more worship teams are inviting the congregation to join with them through overheads or songsheets or whatever, and together they all become the performers, and they all sing to an audience of One. They sing to the Lord. He is the focus. He is the reason for doing it. And with that dynamic, everything changes.

In a performance mode, there is always an element of competition and comparison to the previous group that was up or the group that will be here next week. I doubt that the Lord is pleased with the striving attitude that wants to make the music sound real good so that we are better than the previous group. The motivation is definitely wrong. However, when the mentality is that the congregation is the worship team, it makes for a very healthy atmosphere for those who are leading from the platform. When the congregation joins in, there is a oneness of family, and the element of competition and striving is not there. People don't go home saying, "worship was kind of hot today" or "worship was awful today." Who cares? It wasn't for us. It was for Him. The issue is not performance. The issue here is that we want to please God; therefore, we sing to an audience of One.

If we, as members of the platform worship team, are struggling every time we step off a stage with feelings of how well we did or did not do, we have a problem. Let me just ask you, those of you who are musicians or singers: How many times have you gone on stage and done it perfectly—no mistakes? I can tell you how many times I've done it. Never. On the other hand, you may be struggling with the fact that you are not on a platform worship team.

We must trust God to place us where He wants us. Our calling and placement come from the Lord. He is the One who appoints, and our significance comes from Him, not from what we do for Him.

It's hard, Lord, to get
beyond the performance issues.
Please change my heart and mind.

The job of a worship leader is to do exactly that— lead in worship. As you may remember from an earlier chapter, the best way to lead people in worship is to worship. Unfortunately, many worship leaders carry a weight of responsibility that they should not be carrying. There are hundreds of fabulous worship leaders, and you might listen to their recordings and think, *I can't do this. I can't measure up to this.* The truth of the matter is that you really can't. You can't be somebody else. You need to be who you are in Christ, and that will probably mean that something will always be changing. You are always growing in your walk with the Lord. It's a process.

And listen, there aren't any perfect churches, there aren't any perfect worship leaders, and there aren't any perfect people—except for Jesus. So in the midst of our messes, our needs, and our hurts, and the process of our walk with God, let's relax. Let's quit putting expectations on each other and simply focus on Him.

Let me give you a practical example of this. Every now and again I feel that God doesn't want me to say anything at all between or during songs; not anything. But when I sense this happening, I know that there will be people in the congregation who are expecting me to do something. And so, just to waylay my fears of letting those people down, at the beginning of worship I'll say something like this: "I think God is telling me that He doesn't want to hear from me. He doesn't want me to do any talking tonight, so from this point on I'm not going to say anything. We are just going to flow with the worship and go where He wants to go."

I realize that there are some churches where the leadership wants someone who will take charge in worship and just run with it, and the people love that. They love to be led. They feel very insecure if they are not sure what is happening. Our church may be a little different in that we like the idea of giving a little more space. I have the wonderful knowledge that our congregation will still love me even if I totally mess up and do it all wrong. There is mercy and grace here. I know that they will still love me. They know that I'm not perfect. They know I'm in a process, so they don't lay heavy expectations on me. That means a lot to me.

I think the main reason that we have learned not to lay expectations upon each other is that during the past five years, we have seen over and over again what God can do in the very midst of our inabilities. I remember one night about three months into renewal when one of the pastors casually walked over to me and said, "Hey, Jeremy, what do you think about giving an altar call tonight?" I said, "Sure." We finished worship, and I was just putting my guitar away when that pastor took the microphone and said, "By the way, is there anybody here who would like to become a Christian tonight?"

I was shocked. *By the way?! Couldn't he have at least talked about the blood of Jesus? Couldn't we have at least sung "Just As I Am" or something? This is the worst excuse for an altar call that I have ever heard in my life. This is absolutely pitiful!* Then I watched as about 40 people got up and walked forward. You could have blown me over with a feather. There God was again, doing it by Himself.

Realizing that God can do it by Himself definitely helps to take the focus from our "doing" and put it on our just "being." Who we are, not what we do—that's what God is interested in.

Save me, Lord Jesus, from the busyness of doing that keeps my focus on me, instead of on You.

Worship should be practiced as a lifestyle both corporately in the church and individually at home. In our training sessions I ask, "Do you ever go home and sit in front of the piano or pick up your guitar or even just put on a tape and worship the Lord? Just by yourself? Not to get ready for anything. Just you and the Lord?" What happens on an individual basis has a marked effect on what will happen on a corporate basis. I tell our worship teams that our prayer time before we actually worship is never to be a substitute for the secret history, the closet time, which is so like what David was doing in the tent. That's the time when real worship, truthful worship, occurs. Quiet individual worship at home—just you and Jesus—will have a powerful effect on what happens corporately. Your worship will begin to come out of who you *are*, not out of the external things you *do*.

We say that worship is given solely for God's glory and honor. There is a big period at the end of that. We do not worship so that we can look good. There is a very real danger for those people who are worship leaders. The danger, as John Wimber expressed it, is that you can actually end up worshiping worship.

Much time, energy, and money is spent getting the songs to sound good. When you consider the cost of the equipment and the time spent in preparation and rehearsal, more energy is usually put into preparing the song than into using the song for the purpose it was designed for, specifically, to bring glory and honor to the Lord. We just need to be very careful. The purpose of this is Him. He is what it is all about.

The same concerns also apply in the area of our particular gifting or training. A person's talent or years of instruction can be simply too important to them. For example, what would happen if I trained for 30 years on a piano, and all of a sudden the Lord began moving to acapella music. I would be challenged. We all tend toward building our own kingdoms in some way, and there will always be the challenge of choosing our kingdom or His. I want my heart to be open. Ultimately, it starts with a right heart, doesn't it? A contrite heart.

We need to be very cautious how much we care about our instruments, our equipment, our gifting, or what other people think about us. If any of these become more important to us than the Lord, there is a name for that. Giving attention to people or things when that attention is supposed to be given to the Lord is called idolatry. Of course, idolatry is the last thing we want to be promoting in the midst of our worship services, but it is entirely too possible.

Cleanse me, Lord Jesus, from worshiping worship or the stuff for leading worship.

The investment in musical instruments, public address equipment, sound consoles, amplifiers, etc., etc., etc., can be a bottomless money-sucking pit, and you will still never arrive. It's like when someone asked Rockefeller, who was the richest man in the world, "How much money is enough money?" His answer was, "Just a little more." That's what it is like with public address systems and equipment. There is always some new item on the market that promises to do twice what the present equipment does, at half the price.

Listen, be good stewards of the money that God has entrusted to you. Stuff for leading worship is incredibly expensive. If you are considering investing in sound equipment for your church, get a consultant. The money that you pay that person might very well save you thousands of dollars. Pray for wisdom, and go for quality. Get the equipment that will do the job. Pray for God's covering over every aspect of your church's worship ministry. Guard against "performance orientation" in every area.

Prayer Protection Over the Worship Ministry

After consulting the people, Jehoshaphat appointed men to sing to the Lord and to praise Him for the splendor of His holiness as they went out at the head of the army, saying: "Give thanks to the Lord, for His love endures forever." As they began to sing and praise, the Lord set ambushes against the men of Ammon and Moab and Mount Seir who were invading Judah, and they were defeated (2 Chronicles 20:21-22).

As we read the Scriptures, we understand that when the nation of Israel was going to take a city in battle, the first people who were sent out were the worshipers, making them the first target that the enemy would respond to. Worshipers seem to be particularly vulnerable to attacks in a wide spectrum. They can feel totally worthless like failures, or they can become proud and puffed up.

What we have been doing recently is involving a few more of our people in terms of protection and warfare on behalf of the front line worshipers. A number of our intercessors often stand at the four corners of the stage and pray for us during worship. They are not actually on the stage or in a place of visibility, but they are there to pray and intercede for us. I am really finding a big difference since they have been there to pray. It is much easier to hear God's voice. It has become much easier to flow with His direction now that these wonderful intercessors are standing there with us and doing battle for us.

Let's stop for a moment to consider the attack on worshipers in an even broader sense. Sadly, there has been much greed in the Christian music industry. There are many people who have been trying to build their own kingdoms. But I believe this is changing. I know a number of worship leaders who are crying out, "Father, release a new song in the earth. I want to hear the songs the angels are singing." And their very next prayer is, "But, oh God, don't let me take advantage of it. Don't let me commercialize it."

My dear friend, Dan Cutrona, owns Kle-Toi Records. Dan produces almost all the music coming out of our church here in Toronto, and he also happens to be a pretty awesome keyboard player. One day he said to me, "Jeremy, do you think we could ever round up a bunch of people who would ask God to give them some songs, and not put their names on those songs? We could go into the studio; record the songs with no copyright, no names, not even who produced it; and then just watch God bless it." I like that concept!

I believe that Christian musicians must be very careful in this whole area of performance orientation. The issue again is that we are singing and playing to an audience of One. What people think of us is irrelevant.

Many times I have caught one of our vocalists or musicians shaking his [her] head after worship and saying something like this: "I'm sorry. I sure messed up in that one song today." Each time I remind the person that it was for the Lord, and He was pleased.

We take ourselves far too seriously. Now, I believe in excellence. Don't get me wrong. I believe in giving the best that I have, but I want you to know that even my best is really ratty. It's filthy rags (see Is. 64:6). I will continue to do my best, but the thing I desire most is the presence of the Lord in our worship services. And the presence of the Lord is not dictated to by excellence of music. His presence comes in response to the hearts of the worshipers.

I long for Your presence, Lord, to see You as I worship; to touch Your heart.

Please take a moment to consider how you view your ministry in your church. Is it something that you feel that you have to do because you are expected to perform? Or are you doing it so that you will win God's favor? Listen, you can't make God love you any more than He already does. You need to understand and truly believe that if you did nothing else for the Kingdom of God, He would not love you any less.

Heavenly Father, would You open our eyes and the eyes of our hearts to really see how much You love us. Please let us see the truth that we don't have to win Your approval. Help us to understand that You love us just because we were made in Your image, and if we do nothing else in a tangible way, it won't affect at all Your love for us. Father, thank You for setting us free to minister and do the work of the Church without encumbrance; to be able to do it because we love doing it. We find joy in serving. Let what we give to You please You, Father. Help us to serve from hearts overflowing with love for You.

Thank You, Jesus, for the privilege of Your presence. Thank You, Holy Spirit, for coming in power. Thank You, Father, for Your mercy and endless love. All power, wealth, wisdom, strength, honor, glory, and praise is Yours! We cry, "More, Lord!"

I Will Seek You

(Jeremy Sinnott)

I will seek You, (I will seek You,)
I always will. (I always will.)

With my whole heart,
With my whole life,
With all that I have
I will seek (serve, praise, love) You.

I will serve You, (I will serve You,)
I always will. (I always will.)

I will praise You, (I will praise You,)
I always will. (I always will.)

I will love You, (I will love You,)
I always will. (I always will.)

Chapter 7

Early Days of Renewal

One question that we are asked on a regular basis is, "Why Toronto? Why did God choose to pour renewal upon your church?" I love the response that our pastor, John Arnott, gives to that question. "I wish I could tell you how spiritual we are and how faithfully we prayed," he says, "but this simply was not the case. We didn't do anything to deserve such an outpouring."

We didn't deserve it, but we are certainly thankful! We are thankful for the thousands of Christians who have prayed for revival for many years. We are thankful to be partakers, along with many others, in what God is doing in the earth.

The life message of our church has been the Father heart of God—of mercy and grace and freedom in the Lord. That gentleness is loved, appreciated, and hopefully demonstrated here. Our motto is to "walk in God's love and then give it away." We don't do it perfectly, but that is the heart, the essence, of what we want to do.

As I previously stated, it was definitely a stretch for us to become involved in this style of ministry, and I did so very cautiously. After that first encounter when John borrowed my PA equipment, Connie and I attended their home group meetings for about a year, and we occasionally helped them with the worship. Then, in early 1988, John asked us to be part of the leadership team at the new church that he and Carol were starting, which was then called Toronto Airport Vineyard. It began with Sunday afternoon meetings, which eventually moved to Sunday mornings.

I had been the principal of a local Christian school for 18 years. Two years after the church was born, I began working on staff on a part-time basis. It became increasingly difficult to juggle my responsibilities at the school with the needs of our new and growing fellowship; so in August 1992 I began working in a full-time capacity at the church.

In January 1994 renewal hit. I watched as God turned our nice little church upside down. Up until that point about 350 people attended on Sunday mornings. We had home group meetings and a whole lot of great training programs that were going well. It was all very nice and manageable. Suddenly things changed, and they have never been the same since.

We had invited a gentleman named Randy Clark to conduct three days of special meetings at our church. During the first meeting, to our complete astonishment,

God's power was unleashed upon us in unusual ways. People whom we knew and trusted began shaking, laughing, crying, etc.—all prompted by the Holy Spirit. The next two evenings were the same. We didn't understand, but God kept showing us over and over again that it was really He who was doing all these things. People were being transformed before our eyes as God empowered them. Complacency broke off many as they fell more passionately in love with Jesus. Timid people became bold in the power of the Spirit and were released into new levels in the prophetic realm and in intercession. We began to understand that this was a sovereign move of God.

At the very first meeting, Connie was sitting in the front row. One of the ladies who was praying thought that she had come forward when there was an invitation to be prayed for. Connie politely let her pray. This lady kept praying and praying. It was Connie's first experience of "soaking prayer," where people are prayed with for long periods of time, even hours, while the Father soaks them in His presence. During this prayer time, Connie became aware of a tingling, then a numbness, around her mouth. This increased in intensity until her whole face was paralyzed. It lasted about four hours.

At the end of the time of prayer, Connie found that she couldn't speak. Some people tried to be helpful by giving an interpretation of what was happening: "Perhaps God wants her to be silent and listen to Him." "Maybe she is being anointed to preach." Actually, God showed her that it was a response to her crying out to Him the week before—for something so sovereign and so real that she would know it was Him. The numbness and inability to speak were actually a tender, personal, and very real touch from the Lord. It was God's way of assuring both Connie and me right from the very beginning that what was happening was from Him. He knew that we needed many assurances over the next few weeks as many unusual things took place.

John asked Randy to stay on for more meetings, and over the next few weeks, he spent a lot of time at our church. Later we realized that it didn't matter who was speaking or leading worship; God was moving, and He was the One who wanted all the glory—not any person or group of persons.

John's prayer was, "God, please don't let us get weird." What a waste of breath! People were doing all kinds of weird things, such as falling down, shaking, and bending in ways that were physically impossible except by a sovereign hand. It was chaos. This was certainly not like anything that we would have asked for. We would never have chosen for things to go this way. However, it was so obviously a work of God that we continued to allow Him to do what He wanted, and we tried to keep our hands off.

Give me the wisdom, Holy Spirit, to recognize Your work in people, to give You room to do whatever You want to do.

What we were seeing sent us scurrying to our Bibles to test things according to Scripture. We found some verses, such as Second Chronicles 5:14, where the presence of the Lord came so strongly upon the priests that they could not stand up and perform their duties. There were also several portions of Scripture where angelic beings appeared and people trembled. Some fell down as if they were dead (see Mt. 28:2-5).

There are many other references that mention the effects people experienced as they encountered the presence of God. Some were filled with great joy (see Lev. 9:24; Ps. 16:11; 21:6, etc.). Others wept in His presence (see 2 Chron. 34:27; 2 Kings 22:19). Still others fell down or shook (see Lev. 9:24; Jer. 5:22; Ezek. 38:20).

In our process of searching the Scriptures, we noticed even more bizarre things that God did. Saul of Tarsus was struck down and blinded by the Lord, which resulted in his conversion (see Acts 9:3-9). King Saul in the Old Testament was thrown to the ground, prophesying for a day and a night, which humbled him and prevented him from killing David (see 1 Sam. 19:20-24). Thus, we soon discovered that God certainly isn't limited to doing just what we are comfortable with!

Matthew 7:20 tells us to look for fruit to see if something is from God. So we asked: "What fruit, what good things are being produced in people's lives as a result of what is happening to them?" We also began looking for opportunities to question people who had powerful encounters with the Spirit of the Lord in the meetings. We found that they were saying basically three things.

Their number one response was, "I've never been so in love with Jesus before in all my life. It is like I've just become a Christian all over again."

We have had the privilege of checking back later with a large number of these people. It is one thing for them to say that they're feeling in love with Jesus the day after their encounter with their Lord, or even several days later; but what about the next week, the next month, the next year? We have found that these folks are still in love with Jesus.

The second response from folks who had been powerfully touched was, "I just can't get enough of God's Word." They were voraciously reading Scripture. They were reading not just a verse or two, or even a few chapters, but whole books at a time. And it wasn't just words on a page; it was like the words were written for them. They were just eating it up.

The third thing they told us was, "I just can't wait to get to my neighbors and friends to tell them about Jesus." What God had done in their lives was something they just couldn't stop talking about! In other words, evangelism became a lifestyle for many people around here. It was the most natural thing in the world to talk about what God had done.

We saw these three things happening consistently with people who were doing what we thought to be weird things. I was looking for fruit in their lives, and I certainly found it. Finally, I thought that I might as well jump in too. I began to ask people to pray for me. They would be so sweet, but I felt nothing. Absolutely nothing happened. I didn't even feel dizzy. Our ministry team would pray for me, and no kidding, they would pray for an hour and a half. At the end I would be thinking, *Maybe I should just lie down. They've got to be so discouraged right now. I'm sure that they would feel better if I did something.*

In the end I finally went to John Arnott and said, "John, you may have noticed that I don't fall down or do anything like that." He said, "I noticed that." I said to him, "I do believe this is of the Lord. I've checked it out. I've talked to all these people and I've searched the Scriptures and all the rest. But I have to tell you, there's nothing happening to me."

John then told me to read the second chapter of Acts. I said, "I've read the second chapter of Acts. The Holy Spirit comes in tongues of fire. They speak in tongues and walk around like drunk people. That's the problem—nothing is happening to me!" John just said, "Read on." So I read a little further and caught it.

As we read on in that account, we see how Peter, being full of the Holy Spirit, spoke to a crowd of people clearly, lucidly, and in complete sentences. It was not the ramblings of a drunk man, and 3,000 people responded and gave their lives to Jesus.

You have no idea what that lifted from me. Peter was being supernaturally natural. It was possible—biblically possible. It was at that point that something else clicked with me. I thought of how people are prayed for here. They never pray, "God, please make this person shake; God, please make this person fall down." (I certainly hope that you haven't heard that kind of thing at our church.) The kind of prayers I did hear prayed for me were, "Father, I bless what You are doing, and I pray that You would do a work in Jeremy's heart. Lord, just search out his heart. You know where the needs are. Would You come and meet the needs?"

Incredible change had occurred in my heart over this period of time, and I realized that God had indeed answered the prayers that had been prayed on my behalf. I had never once heard a prayer that said, "Would You please come and make Jeremy shake or fall down or something." But God had been active. He had been doing exactly what we had been praying for all along. He had been working in my heart.

Every night as I lead worship I look around at all the stuff that is going on, and I'm saying, *Lord, could I taste a little bit of that?* But I want you to know that even if I never do, what He has done in my heart, and the changes that have transpired there are sufficient. They are more than sufficient. To this day I still don't shake; I don't fall down; I don't physically feel anything. And my suspicion is that there may be one or two people who are reading this and saying, like I did, "God, don't You love me? What's the matter with me?" Take it from me, He does love you and He will do a work in your heart just like He did a work in my heart. You keep going for it; keep receiving prayer. He is faithful. He loves to respond.

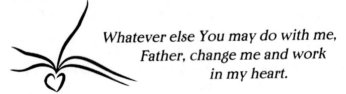

Whatever else You may do with me,
Father, change me and work
in my heart.

In the beginning days of the renewal, our church was absolutely out of control—out of our control, that is. It was wild, and it was glorious. We didn't know how to prepare. I didn't know what songs to do; the music was different every night. Sometimes I wouldn't even know what musicians on the platform would actually be able to play.

We have this one fellow, Joe, who plays keyboard. Joe has a very soft heart toward the Lord. One night I had asked him to modulate between two particular songs. We finished the one song, and I expected to hear Joe making the transition, but there was silence. Okay. Maybe Joe thinks it would be good to have a period of silence at this point. That's great. After a moment or two I thought maybe that Joe had forgotten, so I turned to catch his eye. No Joe. He was out cold on the floor.

Another time we were in a quiet, intimate place in worship and God was all over us. All of a sudden there was a loud combination of all sorts of keyboard sounds right in the middle of the quiet. You just couldn't ignore it. I turned, and there was Joe. He had collapsed on top of the keyboard. His forehead was on the keys. We had to drag him off the stage. Although it is sometimes awkward to work with Joe, I wouldn't have it any other way! I love the way the Lord works through him.

In all these years of renewal, there has been only one service when we lost the whole team. The first person to go was one of the vocalists. She fell forward on to the next level of the platform. This was all so new to us, and I was horrified. Is she dead?! Her foot was still hooked around the monitor, but her hands were still raised in worship. No, she's not dead. She's fine; leave her alone. The next person to go was the guitarist. Now, you would assume this person would have some measure of intelligence; but no, he fell forward—right on top of his instrument! He was fine and so was his guitar. And one by one they went down. It was amazing. I was left, standing there among the debris of God's slaying power. It was wild, wonderful chaos, and we never knew what to expect next.

A few years ago my thinking would have started along the following lines: *If you want God to come, what you do is start with the girl. She has to do a face plant, and make sure that one foot is hooked this way around the monitor. And guitarist—I want you to fall on your instrument. It will be okay. But fall on top of your instrument, because God will come.*

We are so quick to try to get the formula right and work out the program. There isn't a formula, however. The issue is where our hearts are with God. He will respond to the same degree that the passion for Jesus occurs in the hearts of the worshipers. His Word is very clear: We will find Him when we search for Him with *all* our heart. All right. I'm going to search with all my heart.

I want to know You, Lord Jesus.
With my whole heart I'm seeking
You—and only You.

When it came to choosing songs, I would just pray that God would show us what songs He wanted to hear and how long He wanted to hear them. Prior to renewal, I had gotten worship down to somewhat of a routine. You know, about 40 minutes, with a nice balance of slow songs and fast songs. Now I had no idea what to tell the team.

Sometimes we would sing for ten minutes, and other times we would sing all evening. We had no idea what to practice. Plus, there was no time to practice because we were in church every night.

John would tell us to "plan not to plan." He encouraged us to stay loose. He would say things like, "Just because something worked yesterday doesn't mean that it's on God's heart today." We have learned to watch what God is doing in the midst of the congregation and try to flow with Him. It has become a constant search: "Father, what is on Your heart today? What is it that You want to do, and how can I best work with You to facilitate that?" Please understand that I don't feel particularly good at all this. I've got a long way to go. It's a process.

> *Open the eyes of my heart to see*
> *what You are doing.*

In those initial days of renewal, there was a fear that it would end. Every night we would go until the wee hours of the morning because we thought that that night just might be the last renewal meeting. We had meetings every night of the week. They started at 7:30 p.m. and ended somewhere around 3 the next morning. We would grab a few hours of sleep, go in to work at the church, and then go to another service. After a couple weeks of that, we were starting to get real tired. Some of us were even acting rather grouchy.

There came a day when John said, "I don't think this is going to stop. I think that this is God and that it's going to continue. The question is, 'Do we want to be in it for the long haul or the short haul?' " Of course, we wanted to be in it for the long haul. So John said, "Okay, this means that we don't want to get burned out. You will have to guard your time with your family. I want these to be your priorities: passion for the Lord, then your family, and thirdly, your church activity." I thank God for John's wisdom. He said, "I don't want anyone coming to me and saying that their marriage is in trouble or their kids are in rebellion because they haven't been home. Let's get our priorities right. Make sure that you look after your family. If that means staying home instead of coming to church, you'd better do it."

John cut back our time to 60 hours a week. That time was to include our devotional time, our prep time, and home group meetings. It was hard to cut down to 60 hours. Connie and I and the boys would have an evening at home or a day off, and we would turn to each other and say, "What do you want to do?" "Let's go to church!" Church was the most fun place we could think of to go.

Church, fun? May it be so!

We've been in this for about five years now, and church is still our favorite place to have fun. Within our work week, there is lots of mercy and grace. There are times when we are in a conference and we're in church all day and every night. The following week we go a little lighter and spend more time with our families.

We have found it to be very helpful just to say to our spouses and children, "Well, how are we doing? Do you think I'm spending too much time away from home? Are we okay? Are you okay with my going tonight? Do I have your permission?" Their input is very important. The value of the family in John's eyes has given an immeasurable amount of security to our spouses and children because they do not see renewal as some sort of competition against our time with them. They don't resent the renewal; they love it. It is very freeing to know that we don't have to attend every meeting.

How renewal or revival will impact individual lives and families is a real concern to many Christians. They hear about the nightly meetings and wonder how on earth they could ever handle it because they already feel tired and stretched. I think that too many Christians have had difficulty distinguishing between love for the Lord and church attendance, or love for the Lord and ministry. Listen, loving and caring for our families is a very powerful way to demonstrate our love for the Lord. As a pastor or ministry leader, our job description is secondary to providing for our families, although they do go hand-in-hand in many ways. We might provide for our families by working at the church, but our presence at home is of great significance and value to our spouses and children—even when we are not doing anything except just being there.

I'm so busy, Lord.
Teach me how to balance
the responsibilities in my life.

Let me give you a little background regarding our family. Connie and I met each other in the context of music and song, and it has always been a part of our lives. We actually met at a coffee house where I was singing. She was sitting with another guy at the time, and I was dividing the people up into various groups for a song I was leading. It ended up that I said to her, "I'm going to put you in one group," and I said to the guy, "I'm going to put you in another group. I'm going to separate you two." Those were the first prophetic words that I am aware of ever speaking.

I remember when our boys were very young, how we would drag them out to rehearsals and put them on sleeping bags right next to the drums. I'm not kidding—they would fall asleep right next to the drums. We had decided that there was no way we were going to have a quiet home and tiptoe around with our kids. There was going to be music on all the time, and they would learn how to sleep or play right in the midst of it. This made it easy to have practices.

Since our boys were always immersed in song, it was a natural thing for them to pick up an instrument. It was even more so because we've got every kind of instrument around our house. It was just a question of each picking up one that he liked.

Over the years I've tried to be very careful to say, "Watch out that your heart is not won by your instrument. Watch out that you don't get pulled into music for music's sake." That is very easy to do—to play the music for the music's sake. I tell my boys, "There is a higher calling over you. There is a higher calling over your life, and that is to use your music for Him, to use your gifting for an audience of One. There is no greater thing that you can do with your life than to worship the Creator."

I also encourage the boys to pray the same prayer that I constantly pray: "Father, I just need to focus on You. I am not doing this to impress the congregation. I want this to be my act of worship to You. I want to be the best drummer, the best bass player, or the best worship leader that I can be with the gifting that You have given me so that I can bless You." That is the bottom line.

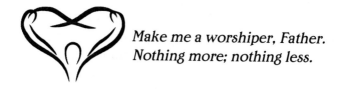

Make me a worshiper, Father.
Nothing more; nothing less.

Shawn, our eldest, is a natural for rhythm. I've always felt that it doesn't matter how many rolls or splashy, fancy things a drummer can do; I mostly want them to keep straight time (which, as I've discovered, is a hard thing for some drummers to do). If they throw some fancy drum rolls in, that's great, but I want them to maintain a steady rhythm. When we saw that kind of steadiness in Shawn, we encouraged him to take lessons. Shawn now plays drums in a number of services each week. In addition to that, he has been working in the resource center here at the church.

When our youngest son, Luke, first picked up a guitar, he was really quite good at it. But as he looked around, it seemed like everybody was playing guitar, so he began to look for another instrument. Bass was very similar, and he picked it up very quickly. What I was most encouraged about was the fact that he took it on himself. That is, he didn't often say, "Dad can you show me this" or that kind of thing. He just watched other people. Luke just loves a challenge. He would put on a CD, listen, play it, then listen and play it again. Luke is presently on staff at the church. He plays bass in many services, and he also works as a chef in the cafeteria.

Our middle son, Trevor, is a worshiper, but the instrument he is gifted in is not a musical one, and the keyboard he uses is not on a piano! Trevor loves working on computers. He spends hours of his time entering data in the church computers and running the computerized system in the sanctuary during services. He is a tremendous blessing, and we are excited to see what God has planned for his future.

There is nothing that does a father's heart more good than to see his children follow the Lord and use their giftings. Each one of our boys is different, and each one has his own talents that God will use without my pushing. I don't want them to be who I want them to be; I want them to flow in their own giftings and talent as they feel comfortable. I want them to really know that both their heavenly Father and their earthly father love them, no matter what. If my children grasp that concept, then it will mean that the stuff that they do in church, the ministry of the church, will be done because they want to do it. They will know that what they do doesn't make any difference at all to how much God or their mom and I love them. They are free to minister just because they want to.

Thank You, Father, for loving me
just because I am.

I think that what I've appreciated the most, and what seems to have ministered deeply to the thousands of guests who have visited us, is the mercy and grace that people have had the freedom to express here. How refreshing it is to realize that our sense of worth is not based on what we do. How refreshing and healing it is to simply realize that the Father loves us.

Lord, thank You for all the things that You've done and for all the times You've come when we've called for more. It was not because we are righteous or because we prayed. It is because of Your mercy and grace. Lord, thank You for all the things You do. Lord, thank You because we know that it's You. Come breathe in us, come make us alive.

With my whole heart, with my whole life, with all that I have I will seek You. I always will.

Do It Again, Lord

(Jeremy Sinnott)

For You alone give life,
You alone are worthy.
You are God Almighty,
You are all we need.
You can save Your church Lord.
You can bring revival.
Lead us up from here,
Do it again, Lord.

Do it again Lord,
Cause us to see.
Do it again Lord,
And set us free.
Let Your fire fall in power,
Let Your joy come with laughter,
Do it again.

Bring Your healing and deliverance.
Let salvation come.
Revive, renew Your church again.

We desire Your presence, as never before.
Lord, come in power, as we ask for more.
Do it again.

Chapter 8

Worshipers in Process

I have the feeling that some of you may have picked up this book looking for new tips to becoming a better worship leader, or you may be wondering how to have a greater sense of God's presence in your worship services. I do hope that by now you have caught my heart in all this and that you have realized the answer is not found in methods. The answer is simply to worship Him, our audience of One. I'm going to assume that this concept is settled in your heart, and at this point I do want to present to you a few practicalities that we have learned in our journey thus far.

Training the Platform Worship Team

Every week the leaders here at Toronto Airport Christian Fellowship are asked a multitude of questions, including: What are the standards for people to be on the platform worship team? What do our training meetings look like? How do leaders handle disciplinary issues? etc.

Of primary importance to me is the fact that I don't want anyone getting his or her identity from being on the platform. I am convinced that fat-headed, star-struck, self-centered worship teams are an offense to the Lord. I want people up on the platform who honor others and love to prefer one another.

I like to say to potential team members, "If you enjoy washing feet, you are going to love being on the worship team; but if you are looking for some prestige or a position of authority, I think God is going to oppose you, and I'm going to help Him." We want to stay small, really small.

I had one electric guitarist, bless him, who had this insatiable desire to jump off the stage at the end of one particular song. Five nights in a row he asked me if he could do this, and five nights in a row I gave him the same answer, "Yes...but not tonight." Finally, he caught on.

I actually want two seemingly opposite things from worship team members. On one hand, I want them to model worship; and on the other hand, I want them to be absolutely invisible.

I don't want the feeling that people on the platform are of more importance than people in the auditorium. We are all members of the congregation. I don't want us to draw special attention to ourselves, and jumping off the stage with a guitar would probably draw some special attention. It also might get someone hurt.

We look for a variety of things in the lives of the platform worship team members, particularly in the area of willingness. We want to see a willingness to be teachable, trainable, and accountable. There needs to be a willingness to receive prayer from others, and a willingness to go back to the congregation and just worship there. These are issues that, if there is an area of unwillingness, will be a source of problems or a way that the enemy can get a hook in somewhere down the road.

As in any relationship, everything can appear to be just fine in the beginning. People start off being cooperative, cheerful, and willing. Then you begin to see each other's messes and issues and hurts. Things surface, and they have to be dealt with. Our training sessions are teaching times, but they are also relational times. Half of the time is spent teaching and the other half is spent praying for each other. We have discovered that it is hard to be dishonest when you are praying, and as you open your heart to the Lord when others are around, you are placing yourself in a very vulnerable position.

We seek to maintain an atmosphere of openness and honesty with each other, recognizing that we will discover some dirty laundry somewhere down the road. It is not an issue of *if* we will, but of *when* we will; and when it happens, how we will respond. There are no perfect worship teams because there are no perfect individuals. We are all in process and we all have our issues. Again, the important thing to me is whether or not a person is willing to deal with the issues.

If I see someone who is working on his particular problem or area of need—he is being open, getting prayer, and being accountable to somebody whom he respects and feels comfortable with—then I don't have a problem with him [or her] being on my team (unless moral issues are involved).

Let me give you an example. One musician on our team had a problem with smoking. It was something that he just couldn't shake. Whenever I would talk to him about it, the willingness was there. He was trying different things and different programs to help him quit. Well, we just kept loving him and encouraging him to deal with the problem. We told him that we were going to continue to love him and allow him to be on the team.

Jeremy! You allowed someone on your worship team who smokes?! Yep. Does that upset you? Sorry about that. Every church will do what they feel is right to do. As for us, we understand that people are in a process and that if we waited until everyone was perfect, we would be waiting a long, long time. (By the way, today he no longer smokes.)

Help me not to make judgments, Lord, as You work out Your purposes in me and in others.

Who are we to say that one person's problem is big enough to disqualify him from the worship team, but another person's problem isn't big enough, and he can continue in his ministry? I don't have the ability to make that distinction. I just know that all sin is offensive to God, and if any man offends in one point, he offends in all (see Jas. 2:10). So let's recognize that we're all sinners, we're all offensive to the Lord. That's exactly why we need Jesus.

Now that this is settled, here we are. We've asked Jesus to come into our hearts, and He is now working that wonderful process in our lives. Why on earth should we want to beat each other up as we submit to the process? Some of us work through it quickly; others of us are a little slower. As long as a person is willing to continue with God's refining process, I'm happy to let him be in a position of ministry.

Rehearsals

It is very important to spend time in rehearsals, and for us, this has been a challenge because the sanctuary is busy all the time. So, what do we do? One of the things we do is arrive an hour or so early to practice introductions, endings, and bridges. We have this probably misguided opinion that if we start together and end together, and even if we do something weird in the middle, but we do it together, we are basically okay. We have the added benefit here that some of our musicians actually work at the church on a part-time or volunteer basis, which makes daytime rehearsals possible.

What about new songs? Generally what I do is give a copy of the tape and the score to whoever is to be on the team the next week. Then I say, "You can take this home and put it on your kitchen counter and not listen to it; then when we do it next week, you can just stand there. *Or* you might want to listen to it and come prepared." This works well for me. In nine years I have yet to find someone who didn't know the song really well. In fact, I often have the opposite problem. Take, for instance, electric guitarists. Now these guys are keen. It is nigh impossible for an electric guitarist to stand there with his guitar in tune and his amp cranked up, and not play.

I like to build songs. I like to start with one instrument and add another instrument in the second verse. I try to explain this to the electric guitarists, "Please listen to me. I want to build this song, so I'm going to add an instrument at a time. Pay attention. I want you to come in on the last chorus so we get that nice build. Tell me what I just said to you." Now I'm thinking that he understands. So then we start the song, and he is standing there, guitar in tune, amp cranked. You can almost see the wheels turning. He is thinking: *A chime would go really well right here.* Bing. *Coming around again.* Bing. *That's beautiful. I could probably get two chimes actually.* Bing, bing. *I could probably get a slide in there. I could probably get a trill in there too.* And I'm standing there with this look on my face: *We are still in the first verse. What are you doing?!* And he is surprised. Bless the electric guitarists, oh Lord.

Going With the Flow

This old phrase takes on a whole new meaning when there is a real flow to go with, when the river of God's presence really is in a meeting and we, as a worship team, are trying to move with Him. In any given worship time, I usually move from celebrative to intimate, and then add a mid tempo at the end. That is the general framework we use, all the while trying to be very open and responsive to what the Father is speaking in that particular service.

I usually have a theme for the meeting, which I have tried to establish after being in conversation with whoever will be speaking, and I make the song list about five days in advance. (I think that God can probably tell me five days in advance what He would like to hear just as well as He can five seconds before we are going to sing it. I don't think that this needs to be an issue. It's not an issue to me, and I don't think it's an issue to the Lord how far in advance you choose a song.)

Once we have the song list, we usually don't deviate from it too much, unless it seems very obvious that God is going a different direction than what we had planned. Until recently, we used overhead projectors; now we've gone to a computerized system, which has helped us immensely. I tend to be highly forgetful. I would always forget to ask someone to run the overhead. Delegation would have been smart, but I would even forget to ask someone to ask someone. I would be up on the platform ready to begin when I would suddenly think: *Is someone ready to put the transparency up? No. Of course not; I forgot to ask!* "Quick! Would you please go down and ask somebody to do overheads? Just grab anybody!"

Some poor person would be sitting there happily thinking about how he got a front row seat—*This is going to be so nice.* Suddenly someone would run up to him, "Quick! Can you do the overheads?!" "Uh...I...sure, well, I guess so. How do you turn it on?" They are willing, but just a bit nervous. "Okay, I see how this works...now you move it up...I get it. Okay, I can do this." And then I change the song list.

So he puts up what he thinks is the next song. *No.* Then he moves it up, thinking that maybe I had started with the chorus. *No.* So the draftee starts flipping through the songs. *Maybe they're in the wrong order.* Little beads of sweat are now forming on his forehead as he starts going through the files of songs, beginning with "A."

You know what the congregation is doing. They are waiting, patient Christians. And that person never sits in the front row again.

It was in those days that we learned to try to keep to the song list, and we put a trained person in charge of the song projection who could quickly recognize any changes.

Drawing People Into Worship

I try to begin every worship service with an invitation for the people to feel at home. I extend freedom to them to be who they are. I also give any instructions and expectations regarding the meeting so that I don't have to stop and say anything later on. My opening words go something like this: "We want to give you lots of room tonight to worship the Lord in a way in which you feel comfortable. You may want to just stay seated in your chair, or on the other hand, you might feel like dancing, clapping, yelling, and shouting—and all those things. I think God likes both. Let's relax tonight, and let's allow each other to be who we are."

Once we actually enter into worship, especially once we've done the exuberant, rowdy, declarative songs and we are into a place of intimacy with the Lord, I don't want to say very much at all. I don't want to instruct the people because that makes them listen, evaluate, and process the instructions. The moment they do that, their focus is off the Lord. Giving instruction in the midst of worship is actually pulling people away from worship. So I want to be very careful that we give our instructions at the beginning. Then we just let it flow.

Now, as we flow, if I reach a point in the meeting when if I don't know what to do, I do nothing. This is my typical encouragement to worship leaders and worship teams: Don't feel pressured to make something happen. Don't get active; back off instead. Just give the Lord and the people some space. Often, in the midst of that position of waiting, the Lord will initiate a particular kind of ministry.

It could be that He prompts you or someone else to say something like, "If you are feeling lonely today would you just slip your hand up? We are going to continue to worship, and I invite those who are around someone who has his hand raised: Would you just quietly pray for the person standing near you?" So in the midst of worship there will be a time of ministry that is very effective. We welcome the ministry of the Holy Spirit in whatever way He chooses.

I want to meet You, Holy Spirit, in whatever way You want to reveal Yourself to me.

I've been asked how to get the congregation more involved in worship. Most of the time I believe that people *want* to worship: The problem is that they don't really know *how.* They have not seen it modeled, or they haven't personalized what they've seen. We need to help folks with this internalization process. We need to constantly remind them that worship is all an issue of the heart, and a lot of it boils down to making choices. Why do we worship? If it's a matter of whether or not we feel like worshiping, our focus is all wrong. Again, we worship because He is worthy.

I have found this to be so important for me personally. I cannot go by my feelings. There have been times when, halfway through the worship service, I'm feeling dry and downright empty. I cry, *"God! Where are You?!"* Then I open my eyes and to my extreme surprise, people will be all over the floor weeping and crying out to the Lord. *"Oh. There You are."* On the other hand, I've also felt a powerful sense of God's presence in a particular service, only to have someone come up to me afterward and say, "Boy, worship was really dry today, wasn't it?"

So, instead of going by my feelings, I've just determined to believe that God is a great big God, and He will accomplish everything He wants to do. He has just asked me to worship. He didn't say that I should worship if I feel like it; He just asked me to do it. If, in that place of surrender and obedience, my emotions happen to get stirred—thank You, Lord. But if my emotions remain in a quiet, dry place, it doesn't matter. I'm doing this for Him, not for me.

More and more often, I find that we are in a place where we actually sense the glory of the Lord. Isn't that the cry of the Church? "Father, we want to see Your glory! We want to see the cloud of Your presence in the middle of our sanctuaries!" We need to teach people what intimacy in worship is all about. We need to encourage them to get their focus off the worship leader and the platform team and onto the Lord. We need to teach them biblical forms of worship and demonstrate those forms.

Biblical Forms of Worship

Instruments

Psalm 150 says this:

*Praise the Lord. Praise God in His sanctuary; praise Him in His mighty heavens. Praise Him for His acts of power; praise Him for His surpassing greatness. Praise Him with the sounding of the **trumpet**, praise Him with the **harp** and **lyre**, praise Him with **tambourine** and dancing, praise Him with the **strings** and **flute**, praise Him with the clash of **cymbals**, praise Him with resounding **cymbals**. Let everything that has breath praise the Lord. Praise the Lord.*

This Scripture encourages us to use a wide variety of instruments in worship. God likes to hear instruments, and do you know that He is not offended by loud music? I'm not saying that we should crank up the PA system and blow off everybody's ears; but what I am saying is that God's ability to receive praise and adoration encompasses the loudest of the loud. I think that it will be incredibly loud in Heaven. We talk about mountains rumbling. There aren't PA systems that can do that. From the loudest of the loud to the quietest of the quiet—silence even—God's ability to receive worship encompasses it all...all of it.

Shouting

> *When the trumpets sounded, the people **shouted,** and at the sound of the trumpet, when the people gave a loud shout, the wall collapsed; so every man charged straight in, and they took the city* (Joshua 6:20).

> ***Shout** for joy to the Lord, all the earth, burst into jubilant song with music; make music to the Lord with the harp, with the harp and the sound of singing, with trumpets and the blast of the ram's horn—**shout** for joy before the Lord, the King* (Psalm 98:4-6).

Shouting is a form of warfare. It brought down the walls of Jericho. There is a place for being loud and rowdy. There is a place for singing our declarative songs where we say, "God, You are great, You are awesome, You are mighty. We have a legal right to be in this place proclaiming what we are proclaiming!" I love it. This sets the groundwork and the framework on a legal basis for what we are doing. And there is something in the heavenlies that occurs as a result.

Clapping

> *Clap your hands, all you nations; shout to God with cries of joy* (Psalm 47:1).

Clapping is also a form of worship. Most churches have come to accept hand clapping in their worship services. Can I encourage you to take it a step farther than simply keeping beat to the fast songs? Try clapping your hands in applause to the Lord. It is a powerful expression of worship to Him. Clapping is also a spiritual weapon that can be used in warfare against the enemy.

Dancing and Leaping

*Then Miriam the prophetess, Aaron's sister, took a tambourine in her hand, and all the women followed her, with tambourines and **dancing**. Miriam sang to them: "Sing to the Lord, for He is highly exalted. The horse and its rider He has hurled into the sea"* (Exodus 15:20-21).

*As the ark of the Lord was entering the City of David, Michal daughter of Saul watched from a window. And when she saw King David **leaping** and **dancing** before the Lord, she despised him in her heart* (2 Samuel 6:16).

Leaping and dancing. Now I know that some of you come from churches where, if you began to leap and dance, you would be escorted leaping and dancing out the door. There has always been a measure of controversy concerning dancing. Perhaps you recall way back in Chapter 3 where I mentioned the confrontation between King David and his wife Michal over this issue.

At our church, although there have been times when we invite people to come forward and rejoice at the front, we generally encourage dancing to be done at the back or the side of the room. There is a lot of space there, and nothing the dancers do will distract other people from worshiping. If someone begins to dance at the front, one of our ministry team will usually ask the dancer a test question. Yes, it is a test. The question is, "Would you mind dancing at the back of the auditorium?"

If he or she says, "I'd be delighted to dance back there," then the ministry team member will probably say, "Oh, never mind, you are doing great right where you are. Keep going for it." But if there is some resistance, it might indicate that the person feels a need to be seen by the congregation. Maybe not, but it might indicate that need. Then the worship team member will sit down beside the dancer and just begin to explain where the team and the church are coming from.

We do believe in dancing, but our dancing is for the Lord. That must be the heart motivation. We are not performing for people; He is our audience, and He can see us just as clearly in the back as He can at the front.

Lifting Hands

Put all these in the hands of Aaron and his sons and wave them before the Lord as a wave offering (Exodus 29:24).

May my prayer be set before You like incense; may the lifting up of my hands be like the evening sacrifice (Psalm 141:2).

Lifting, stretching, and waving our hands are biblical forms of worship. Some people love to raise their hands to the Lord, but others feel very uncomfortable about it. I remember what happened the first time I determined to raise my arms in all-out worship to the Lord. I walked in the door thinking, *This is the day, Lord. I'm going to worship You with everything I have in total abandonment and total freedom.* As we began to worship it was like this: *One, two, three—well, I have most of my fingers up.* My heart was soaring, but I felt that everybody in the congregation was looking at me. I was very self-conscious. And that was the problem: I was self-conscious, and not God-conscious.

There's that heart motivation thing again. Our measure of spirituality is not gauged by how high our hands are. God is always looking at our hearts, and I would be wise to do the same. When I notice people with their hands in their pockets, I want to be careful to say, "It's okay to do that. Please be free to keep your hands by your side. If you find worshiping sitting down is easier, please sit down. If you find worshiping is easier when you dance, please dance. Be you. Be who you are. Just be sure that your focus is on Him."

Kneeling

Come, let us bow down in worship, let us kneel before the Lord our Maker (Psalm 95:6)

What about kneeling? To those of you from Anglican and Catholic congregations, on behalf of churches like mine, thank you. Thanks for showing us that kneeling can be a natural, normal part of the whole service. I never knew that. No kidding. I never knew that. I thought that kneeling was reserved for the end of the service when you came forward and knelt before the altar; but kneeling can be much more than that. What happens when we kneel? Really, we are humbling ourselves, aren't we? Did you know God gives lots of grace to the humble (see Prov. 3:34)? Do you want lots of grace? I want as much as I can get. Let's be quick to humble ourselves before the Lord.

Falling Down

When all the people saw this, they fell prostrate and cried, "The Lord—He is God! The Lord—He is God!" (1 Kings 18:39)

What about falling down? Now I'm not talking about the falling down where the presence of the Lord comes and you can't stand up. What I'm talking about is making a decision to actually lie face down on the floor. I have yet to meet anyone who has chosen to do that and has not been powerfully impacted by God. Now I realize that if some of you did that in your church, the ambulance would be called, oxygen masks would be set over your face, and they would haul you out. However, that is not the case around here. We are more than used to stepping over and around people on the floor. If this is not a comfortable thing to do at your own church, that's fine; but if you feel that the Lord is asking this from you, do it at home. Let's be worshipers. Let's prostrate and lower ourselves before Him.

Singing

Worship the Lord with gladness; come before Him with joyful songs (Psalm 100:2).

Our worship is directed to and focused on God. We just don't sing *about* God, we sing *to* Him. There is a marked jump in intimacy when we sing to Him rather than about Him. Check it out in your own heart the next time you are in a worship setting.

May my song be to You, my God.
May my heart's desire be to see
and please You.

When we are looking for new songs to teach the congregation, we draw from every source that we can, the old hymns, professionally published selections, and home-grown originals. We are interested in any song that is personal and intimate with the Lord. Today there is a deluge of fabulous songs. Everybody is writing wonderful songs. Fifteen years ago, in my personal opinion, I could count on one hand the songs that I thought were really good Christian songs. That was just how I felt. Today I can't keep up. I can't keep up with just listening to the songs that are wonderful, let alone learning them.

Generally what we do is to begin the meeting with highly celebrative, declarative songs that just establish who we are and what we are doing. This helps the people to focus, and it also has an impact on the enemy. Things will break in the supernatural realm on the basis of our declaring who we are in Christ and what He has done for us. I find that there is usually an anticipation in the people at the beginning of the service. They want to dance and celebrate, so let's do that.

Although our worship may be emotional, we don't want to work up emotions. We actually want to dial down in our worship. I want to get to the place of intimacy. I love our celebrative songs, and there needs to be a place for praise and high celebration, but where I want to go is to that quiet place with the Lord. I can't hear God very well in the loud rowdy songs. I hear Him a lot better in the quiet songs.

Free me, Holy Spirit, to worship
with all my being;
but keep me from emotion
for emotion's sake.
Draw me into that place where

*it is just You and me
face to face.*

If we end worship at that really intimate spot, it is hard to do anything else. It is rude to give announcements at that point. Yet we usually need to move on, so what can we do? If in your liturgy—and every church has one—you want to go into testimonies or the sermon or something, we have found that if you just bring a mid tempo song in, it gently brings people out of the deep worship, and the leaders are able to take the congregation into whatever other areas the liturgy requires. If, however, you want to remain in that intimate place, either remaining silent or moving into a time of ministry can be very effective.

We have noticed some interesting dynamics. We have noticed, for instance, that when the presence of the Lord has come down during worship, you can stop playing between songs and just have it quiet, and the Holy Spirit will remain. You can sing a song—a prophetic song or tongues or something like that—and the Holy Spirit will remain. You can pray in the middle of a song or between songs, and as long as you pray to God, the Holy Spirit will remain. "As long as you pray to God?" you may ask. "Who else are you going to pray to?" Let me explain.

If I pray, "Father, thank You for Your presence here. We just welcome You to come and touch us and do a work in our hearts," He will. He loves to respond to that kind of invitation. But if I pray something like this, "Oh God, these people are so slow to worship, I've never seen such miserable worshipers in my life.

Would You come and do something to them?!" That will shut worship down real quick.

Notice what is happening. The moment we take our focus off Him, His presence begins to lift. It is a very simple issue. Therefore, any exhortation, instruction, or teaching that I want to give to the congregation needs to happen before we reach that place in the meeting.

During the time of ministry when people are receiving prayer, we just want to sing quiet intimate love songs to Jesus. I don't want the prayer team to have to shout in people's ears to be heard. At least, I hope that's the case. It is hard for me to hear on stage how loud it is out in the congregation. But I want it to be quiet enough so that people can carry on a normal conversation and receive prayer. God often uses the intimate songs to touch people's hearts in a very personal way.

We have discovered that as long as we worship, ministry to the people flows much more easily. God inhabits the praises of His people (see Ps. 16:11 KJV). As I stated in an earlier chapter, we have discovered that the Holy Spirit knows the difference between live worship and a CD. So do people. On any given night, it is somewhere around 11:00 when the worship team finishes. I've noticed what happens when the soundman puts a CD on. He does his best to make it a smooth transition. It is the same song at the same volume, but you will immediately sense the Holy Spirit begin to lift, and people turn to each other and begin talking. It happens every single night. There is just something about the heart involvement within live worship. So, during the prayer and ministry time in your own church, let me encourage you to have at least one person up front to actually worship.

A few years ago, I felt prompted by the Holy Spirit to quietly step off the stage with my guitar and headset microphone, and walk among the people as they were prayed for, singing and ministering as I went. This seemed uncomfortable at first, but now it is what I do on a regular basis. I try to be as unobtrusive as possible. Sometimes I sing whatever prayer I feel the Lord wants over a person; sometimes I sing a song the congregation can join in on. Connie and a few other members of the team have taken to the "wandering minstrel" role as well. Once we have more wireless headsets, I would really like to see the whole team (with the exception of keyboard players and drummers, of course) free to minister this way. I love the fact that we aren't a long distance away on the platform, but we're down where we can actually touch and pray for individuals.

We have also discovered that as people are waiting for prayer, if they will also worship, God will often bring a healing and do work in their hearts while they are waiting. Our ministry team is invaluable in ministering the love of God. Their primary function is to bless what God is already doing, so they look for people to pray for who are already being touched by the Lord. Members of the ministry team are well aware that it is not human words that are needed. People who have come for prayer need to have God respond to their cries.

I pray that what we have learned will be of use to you in your setting, but please do understand that there are no formulas. The whole issue really rests upon where our hearts are. How God responds is relative to the degree to which our hearts passionately seek after Him. Jeremiah 29:13 promises that we will find Him when we search for Him with all our hearts.

Father, none of us are exempt from the call to be worshipers. It is the first and greatest commandment to worship You with all our heart, mind, soul, and strength. I thank You for the continual process we are in. Thank You that You are leading us all to a closer relationship with You in worship.

Father, I bless those individuals whom You have called to be on platform worship teams. I ask for an increased psalmist anointing over them right now; an increased ability to play their instruments, an increased ability to sing for You. Father, give them hearts that are right before You, hearts that are filled with love for Jesus. Increase the prophetic anointing in their lives, Lord, and let intercession rest over them so that they might know Your heart, Your desires, Your joys, Your sorrows....

In the name of Jesus, I now sanctify you as a worshiper. I sanctify you and set you apart for Kingdom purposes that are high and lofty, for purposes that are noble and carry awesome responsibility. I pray that your music will never be just the playing of an instrument or the singing of a song. I pray that God will use your worship to usher in the very presence of the Lord. Amen.

The Son of Man Appears

(Connie & Jeremy Sinnott)

I love the way Your light breaks forth;
Just like the dawn of Your coming.
I love how quickly healing appears;
Your righteousness before us.

Behold the Son of Man appears;
Behold our King is coming!
The Lord will rise upon us;
His glory still increasing!

All glory, all power, all praise is Yours!

You'll come with all Your holy ones;
You'll come in power and glory.
The sky will roll back just like a scroll;
The Son of Man victorious!

Conclusion

Arise, shine, for your light has come, and the glory of the Lord rises upon you. See, darkness covers the earth and thick darkness is over the peoples, but the Lord rises upon you and His glory appears over you. Nations will come to your light, and kings to the brightness of your dawn (Isaiah 60:1-3).

This portion of Scripture is familiar to most of us. I invite you to read it again, this time in the context of worship. The closer we get to the endtimes, the more His glory will shine in our worship services. There is great significance in the fact that during the last ten years or so worship has intensified. The songs that we are singing these days are filled with a new passion and anticipation. There is an expectancy in the air. The sun has begun to rise, and we are in the stages of the dawning. We are starting to experience His glory in worship like never before. His presence is going to increase until finally He Himself will be in our midst and we will be in His presence totally from then on.

I feel that those of us who have the role of worship leaders have an incredible responsibility now—not to do more, but to just rest in His presence and let *Him* do more. The more we get out of the way, the more we can let *Him* make things happen! *But how do we do this? How do we let God move in? How do we let Him take over? How do we let His presence come? How do we facilitate opening up a way for His presence to come?* To me, this is all a very exciting pilgrimage.

God has led us through different seasons, different stages of renewal, because He is taking us somewhere. I believe that the endtime is rapidly approaching. We don't know when it is going to be, but we all have a sense that it is a lot closer than it was a few years ago, or even yesterday. We are closer. God is calling our hearts into deeper intimacy with Him, into deeper experiences of His presence and His glory in our lives.

His glory is arising upon *you*, not just upon the Church as a whole, but upon you as an individual. As the darkness is getting darker and more blatant, the light is getting increasingly bright. Very soon people aren't going to be able to stand in the gray areas any more. There won't be gray areas to stand in! The light will be so obvious. Isaiah tells us that nations will come to us because of the brightness of our light—because of the dawning of the light of His glory upon our lives.

Destination Harvest

In Isaiah chapter 60 we read,

Nations will come to your light, and kings to the brightness of your dawn....the wealth of the seas will be brought to you, to you the riches of the nations will come (Isaiah 60:3-5).

God has a destination in mind for His Church; He is bringing us to the great, end-time harvest of souls. At our own church in the past five years, upward of 20,000 people have become Christians. In Pensacola, Florida, in excess of 100,000 people have given their lives to Jesus. In China, every single day, 35,000 people make a decision for Christ. The figure of what God is doing worldwide, largely by Himself I might add, is at 172,000 people each day who are giving their lives to Him. We stand in amazement and say, "Go, Lord, go! And, Lord, can I be a small part of this?"

Renewal Is Not Our Final Destination

Here in Toronto, and in churches around the globe that are moving in seasons of renewal, you will hear the common cry of "More, Lord!" We are determined in our hearts not to cling to what God is doing right now—because what He is doing right now is not His final destination for us; it is only a place we are passing through along the way. We have not yet arrived. God has much, much more ahead for His people, and we have a definite sense that wherever He wants to go will be even more exciting than where He's already taken us.

And of the children of Issachar, which were men that had understanding of the times, to know what Israel ought to do... (1 Chronicles 12:32 KJV).

[Jesus said] *You know how to interpret the appearance of the sky, but you cannot interpret the signs of the times* (Matthew 16:3b).

We must have an understanding of the times and seasons that God is leading us through. This is so important. If we don't understand, we are not going to cooperate with Him, and tragically, we might even find ourselves fighting against Him. We need to pray like Paul did in Ephesians 1:18, that the eyes of our understanding will be opened. We need spiritual discernment to see what God is doing, both corporately and individually. He is doing some things in your life right now, and it's really important that you seek the Lord and find out what on earth He's up to, so that you can cooperate with Him! And corporately, we need to be in a position of saying, "Lord, make us ready! What do we need to do to cooperate with what You are doing?"

Let me give you an example. When renewal first hit our church, people responded to God with a lot of outward manifestations—laughing, crying, shaking, etc. This was all brand-new to us, but eventually, we got used to it. (And, of course, getting used to something God does is not a good idea.) Then there was a season where we noticed fewer outward physical manifestations taking place. When people were ministered to, many of them would simply rest gently in the Spirit.

At first, it appeared to us that the power level had died down, but then we began to hear testimonies of what God had been doing in people's lives. We heard statements like, "There was such a deep healing that happened in my heart! God took me back to painful childhood memories. He released the pain that I've carried for years! The heaviness inside is gone, and I feel free!"

Sometimes there's a very, very deep inward work of the Holy Spirit occurring while outwardly it doesn't look like a lot is happening. And then, on the other hand, there are times like at one ladies' conference I recall a few years ago—it was what I would call wild.

Four thousand ladies who had been held back and bound up for so long tasted freedom in Christ. When that happens, look out! There were lots of feelings being released, and I remember thinking, *Oh, there's more flesh here than I normally see.* I thought that it was coming from being hyped or whatever, but I did recognize a very healthy emotional release. Then I watched as the scene moved from that sense of emotional chaos to 4,000 women on their knees in total silence. Gradually, from the silence arose deep, heart-rending sobs. All that could be heard for half an hour was intense weeping. God was doing something very sovereign: He was taking those ladies through a time of real repentance. What a powerful meeting that was. I was impacted by God's orchestration and the corporate response from that number of people.

We need to find out, "Lord, what do You want me to do right now? What stage do You want to take me through?" Some of the stages aren't easy; some of them are even painful. But it's important for us to go through each stage in order to get to the next one. If we truly want God's glory to come the way we say that we do, it's really important for each of us to examine ourselves and find out where are we at.

Father, where are You leading me to?
What are You taking me through right now?

Recently, on a global scale, we have seen the Lord taking His people through seasons of intercession. It is vitally important that we get involved in what He is doing. We must be part of this season of intercession and travailing prayer so that we can be part of what God will birth through it.

In John 5:19, Jesus said,

> *I tell you the truth, the Son can do nothing by Himself; He can do only what He sees His Father doing because whatever the Father does the Son also does.*

That is how we want to live. We want to see what the Father is doing, and be involved in that.

In Exodus 33:15, Moses said that unless God was with the Israelites, they didn't want to go anywhere! I say, "Amen, Moses!" And in the context of worship, we want to be sure to keep up with the Lord. We must be careful not to stop and get comfortable in a place that He intends only to be a step along the way. He may take us through times and seasons of celebration, intimacy, repentance, intercession, etc., in our worship. We must continually be open to the new things He wants to lead us into.

Destination Worship

Worship is our final destination; it is where we are going. It's what we will be doing for eternity. Have you ever thought about how long eternity is? Let me help you with this. Imagine, if you will, a mountain 1,000 kilometers wide, 1,000 kilometers deep, and 1,000 kilometers high. Of course, there aren't mountains that big anywhere, but please just imagine it anyway. Now suppose that a little bird comes over, lands on the mountain, and sharpens his beak. The bird flies away for 1,000 years, and when he comes back, he sharpens his beak. When that mountain has been worn away to one grain of sand by that little bird who comes once every 1,000 years to sharpen his beak, that is the first day of eternity.

We have no idea how long this is. This is incredibly long. I used to wonder if worship wouldn't start to get a little boring, but then I realized that our God is absolutely infinite. It doesn't matter how many eternal days we have. There will always be something new to discover about Him for which we can worship Him!

First Corinthians 13:12 says that we see through a glass darkly. Our vision is obscure, and even though He is not clear to us, we still love to worship. What will it be like face to face? Indescribable. Worshiping Him will be our joy, our delight, and our reason for being. That is our final destination, and right now we are on a wonderful, wonderful journey—a pilgrimage in getting to know the Father, our audience of One.

Father, may You receive all the glory and honor that is due Your name! May the name of Jesus be highly exalted! May Your Holy Spirit inhabit the praises of Your people now and forevermore! Amen.